About the Book

They that wait includes poetry written since the mid 60's. Although I had written some poems previously, it was at that time I began to be inspired and my poetry took on new meaning for myself and for those to whom they were directed. There are several poems in the area of faith and commitment that have resulted from my own Christian growth experiences; and a number of poems relating to love of family members. I have always felt that God was able to use me to touch the lives of many people and only recently felt led to put poetry in book form, prayerfully hoping they will continue to reach out to other readers.

They that wait

Poetic Reflections
by
Mollie R. Pool

Inspiring Voices
A Service of **Guideposts**

Inspiring Voices books may be ordered through booksellers or by contacting:

Inspiring Voices
1663 Liberty Drive
Bloomington, IN 47403
www.inspiringvoices.com
1-(866) 697-5313

Because of the dynamic nature of the Internet, any web addresses or links contained in
this book may have changed since publication and may no longer be valid. The views
expressed in this work are solely those of the author and do not necessarily reflect the views
of the publisher, and the publisher hereby disclaims any responsibility for them.

Any people depicted in stock imagery provided by Thinkstock are models,
and such images are being used for illustrative purposes only.

Certain stock imagery © Thinkstock.

ISBN: 978-1-4624-0645-6 (sc)
ISBN: 978-1-4624-0644-9 (e)

Library of Congress Control Number: 2013909306

Printed in the United States of America.

Inspiring Voices rev. date: 5/21/2013

TABLE OF CONTENTS

Acknowledgements

Since my serious writing began by inspiration from God, He is first and foremost to be acknowledged. Anything worthwhile I have written has within it "the touch of the Master's hand."

As is always the case, it is close family and friends who give one the most support and encouragement—my husband, children, grandchildren and close friends have been there for me through and through.

There's another wonderful group—a "cloud of witnesses"—who have gone before. I continually sense their love and presence in all I say and do . . . their influence never ends! The final chapter includes some odes and eulogies to these instruments of God's love and peace. Writings for two wonderful members of this group are missing—Lowell Myers, brother-in-law, and Clyde Pool, father-in-law. Both were wonderful father figures and played significant roles in my life, and both went to be with the Lord prior to my "serious" writing days. I am forever grateful for their influence!

Foreword

Once I Was Blind

Queried by the Pharisees regarding the conditions of his healing and identity of the Master, the blind man knew no answers but only could say, "One thing I know, that though I was blind, now I see." Physical blindness is perhaps the worst affliction to be saddled with in human existence; therefore, we are thrilled to hear how Christ healed the blind and live in the hope that such afflictions will be lifted in heaven. However, there are other kinds of blindness with which many humans are afflicted in this life attributable to our lack of communication with God and our inability to understand His perfect will for our lives. I was so afflicted.

All my life I have been a "dabbler" in the arts. With a concert violinist father, I managed to learn enough violin to play in the junior high and church orchestras, but quit before I could play well. My older sister became an accomplished pianist and teacher, but I quit piano lessons before I was skilled enough to utilize that talent profitably either, for myself or for the Lord. I took voice lessons in college desperately hoping, in vain, to become a member of its top choral groups. Endowed with some artistic ability in drawing, lettering, etc., again I never developed these talents fully enough to make them useful to any great degree. As a young teen, I was always spellbound by the evangelistic artists and dreamed of some day being used of God through my art.

In my mid 20's, I began to feel I had failed God by not nurturing the talents He had planted within me. At that time, a happy wife of a very busy husband, the mother of three active children, and a working mother to boot, I had very little time to myself, let alone time to spend taking lessons or working on hobbies.

It was at about this point in my life when I began to write some simple poetry "just for fun"—rhyming words to the delight of my friends and relatives to lift their spirits and make them laugh. The more I wrote, the more people asked me to write, particularly for special occasions. Writing for fun . . . I was blinded by the thought that that's where it began and that's where it would end.

It was on a Friday. My school teacher husband came home from the final day of an ordinary week after having had a lengthy discussion with his principal regarding Bible truth. This man had made light of the Bible stories, referring to them as legends or tales to make Scripture more interesting. We discussed this conversation over dinner along with other things, and it was soon lost in flippant chatter and family discussion.

On Sunday morning as I was listening to someone's solo in church, my mind began to wander and I thought of this principal's lack of faith in the Scripture. Suddenly, the happenings of that morning worship service were gone from my presence, and I found myself in a different world. Words—beautiful, poetic words—of response began to flow through my mind, and I quickly grabbed a pencil and paper and began to write. For the first time my life, my blinded eyes were opened! I finally realized that God could inspire a man to use what simple, small talent he possesses to fulfill His purpose on earth. I believe God's purpose in this revelation to me was two-fold:

- Even though I had always believed that Scripture was true, I questioned exactly what was meant by "inspired." What a revelation—that His words should flow through <u>even me</u>!

- God is able to use my life and my limited ability to enlighten those around me.

Now I, like the blind man, respond to those asking questions, "I can't tell you how, I can't answer all your questions, I can only tell you that once I was blind, but now I see!"

My first inspired poem, "Jonah and the Whale," was only the beginning of wonderful things to come as God and I became co-workers.

They that wait upon the Lord shall renew their strength.
They shall mount up with wings like an eagle;
they shall run and not be weary,
they shall walk and not faint.
Isaiah 40:31

Jonah and the Whale

I heard a man ask the question,
"Was Jonah really swallowed by a whale?"
And, laughing, he muttered unbelievingly,
"Just a legend, an old Bible tale."

My mind began to ponder
As I traced Bible history;
Did God create the universe,
Adam and Eve, and you and me?

Was Joseph sold by his brothers
To become an Egyptian slave?
Did he really become a leader?
And later his family did he save?

Did Moses see a burning bush,
And lead Israelites through the Red Sea?
Did Noah really build an ark,
Saving two animals each and his family?

Did Shadrach, Meshach and Abednego
Walk through the fire safe and sound?
Was Daniel protected in the lion's den?
Did David kill the giant while Philistines stood 'round?

Were prophets sent to carry a message
That the world might turn from sin?
As time passed on, did their words prove true,
As people turned from God again and again?

Did God choose Mary, a virgin girl,
To bear His beloved Son?
And did the wise men follow a star?
Did the shepherds hear the angels and come?

Jonah and the Whale (continued)

Did Jesus walk on this sinful earth
And cause the blind to see?
Did He make the lame to walk again,
And cure those with leprosy?

Was He crucified upon the cross,
And did He then rise from the dead
So that we might receive salvation
And by His spirit be led?

Somehow I question not these "tales,"
All a part of Bible history;
Seems not much different at all
From our own country's past to me.

Was George Washington really the Father
Of our own great country?
Did Abraham Lincoln give a Gettysburg Address?
And were the slaves set free?

I believe it all, it was written down
By those who saw and heard;
So historians today watch and observe,
Then begin to write word by word.

And you know, the great God I love and serve
Is omnipotent in His power.
I cannot question His ability to perform
Any miracle at any hour.

He performed the greatest miracle of all
When He saved this soul of mine;
And He who can erase sin from the soul
Can do anything, at any time.

Reflections
on
Faith and Commitment

An Instrument of God's Love

I am an instrument of God's love,
An earthen vessel in the potter's hand.
He molds me daily by His power;
He leads me by His holy plan.

Day by day He clears the hidden path,
Sheds light where I could not see before;
Tunes my heart to make my music sweet,
Asking only that I be His open door.

. . . An open door to share His love for man;
. . . An open door to carry out His plan;
. . . An open door His commandments to fulfill;
. . . An open door to do His Holy will.

Evangelism Explosion

Eternal life's the gift of God,
A gift not to be spurned.
By grace you're saved through faith, my friend,
It can't be bought or earned.

All we like sheep have gone astray,
Ourselves we cannot save.
The wages of our sin is death,
No vict'ry o'er the grave.

Our merciful Heavenly Father
Wants life for one and all;
But sin must needs be punished
As a result of Adam's fall.

For God so loved this sinful world
His only Son He gave
To die upon a cruel cross
That His people He might save.

So look, my friend, to Jesus.
Let Him enter your heart's door.
Trust your life into His keeping,
He's just what you're looking for.

Feed My Sheep
John 21:15-17

Said Jesus to Simon Peter,
"Do you love me more than these?"
"Yes, Lord, you know I love you," said Peter,
Falling to his knees.

Jesus said, "Feed my lambs."

A second time Jesus asked him,
"Simon, do you really love me?"
"Yes, Lord," said Peter, "you know I love you,"
Thinking 'twas easy to see.

Jesus said, "Feed my sheep."

"Do you love me?" asked Jesus the third time,
And this grieved Peter so,
"Lord, you know everything," he cried,
"I love you, and you must know!"

Jesus said, "Feed my sheep."

Give as to You Is Given

Give as to you is given
With a heart overflowing with love.
Forgive as you are forgiven
By Jesus, the Savior, above.

Have You Lost Your Cutting Edge?

In your relationship with Jesus Christ,
Have you lost your cutting edge?
Instead of striving for the prize,
Is your faith hangin' on the ledge?

If you've lost your love for God and man,
How'd it happen, where and when?
Were you distracted, disobedient, prideful,
Careless, or lazy now and then?

Leap from that ledge, express your faith,
Reach out, receive God's touch!
Change the way you think and act,
Let go of what's in your clutch.

Go back to where you first began,
Do those things you did at the first.
Troubled waters then become quite still,
And quenched, your hunger and thirst.

You'll find comfort in the nearness of God,
Loving kindness for every man;
Joy and peace in your salvation,
Fulfillment in seeking God's plan.

(Based on sermon by Rev. Robert Morrison, Nazarene Church Pastor—OH
"Recovering Your Lost Spiritual Vitality," Revelation 2:4-5)

He's Such a Good Young Fella

"He's such a good young fella,"
I heard the pastor say
To Johnny's proud father.
It was just the other day.

"He comes to church each Sunday,
He sits right down in front,
Sings in the children's choir—
What more could a father want?

"He studies hard the questions,
Helps keep the quiz team up.
Why, I'll bet he'll help to earn us
This season's quiz team cup!"

What would they think if they knew
Who the real "Johnny" is
When he puts away his Bible
And forgets about the quiz?

What if they could see him
As he lives his life at school?
Would they be surprised to find
He breaks the Golden Rule?

Would they be proud to see him
Cheating on his tests,
Scrapping in the school yard,
Writing graffiti on the desks?

While Christians may not see us
Beyond the church's door,
Others watching daily know
Just who we're living for.

And God, who's always present,
Sees and hears everything—
The 1st thru 7th days of the week,
Summer, fall, winter and spring!

I Believe in Angels

There's a host of Heavenly angels
The Bible tells me so;
Who watch o'er all God's children
As they travel to and fro.

Sometimes we wonder where they are
Or when they'll come our way.
Are they with me when I'm lost?
Are they present when I pray?

And God has human angels
Who care for one another.
They go about doing good;
All humanity is their brother.

Do I believe in angels?
Is their existence true?
Yes, I believe in angels,
'Cause I believe in you!

I Cannot See Beyond Today

Will my future be sunshiny or gray
With much work to do or much time to play?
Will I be high on the mountain, or in the valley low?
Will the winds be tempestuous, or the breezes calmly blow?

Will I encounter smooth or rugged terrain?
Will I be feeling comfort or pain?
Will my body be weak, or will it be strong?
Will my days be short, or will they be long?

I cannot see beyond today
To know what lies ahead;
But I can trust in Jesus,
For He this life has tread.

He shares my joys and sorrows,
He knows my every care.
He bore upon the cross my sin,
And He's with me everywhere.

I Dare Not Say I Understand
(Proverbs 3:5)

I dare not say I understand exactly how you feel.
Not having traveled down that road, what's ahead I can't reveal.
But rather, friend, than studying a physician's "human" chart,
We're admonished in Proverbs, "Trust in the Lord with all your heart."

And, when the tests and pills and stuff the nurses to you keep handing,
That beautiful verse continues, "Lean not to thine own understanding."
When the days seem long and the way seems dim,
Remember, "In all thy ways" to "acknowledge him."

Then, here's the punch line that this promise has,
The Lord, Jesus Christ, "He will direct your paths."
Cast your burden on Him, He will set you free.
Declare, "I can do all things through Christ who strengthens me."
  (Philippians 4:13)

While I haven't traveled your way before, I've stumbled a time or two;
And, laying my burden at His feet, I've found His promises true.
Only Jesus really understands exactly how you feel;
He's traveled down that road before, and your way He can reveal.

Is God to Blame?

We live in a world filled with turmoil,
Much fighting, hatred and strife.
Violent storms cause much heartache
And devastation to many a life.

We see children abused by their parents,
Sexual abuse by very sick men;
World leaders hungry for power,
Starving their people again and again.

Alcohol and drug abuse abound,
Murders, rapes, thieves in the night;
The innocent so often the victims,
Just how can we make things right?

Is God to blame? Where are you, God?
Why don't You get involved?
If You would just lift Your hand,
These problems could be solved!

Omnipotent and Omniscient--
God is all powerful and wise;
And, yes, He's Omnipresent—
In every facet of our lives.

But He is not some puppeteer
High up there in the sky,
Moving all the strings around
The winds and waves to defy.

Is God to blame? No, I'm to blame,
I am His hands, His feet;
I can be His special instrument,
I must His will complete!

Is God to Blame? (continued)

When God placed us on the earth
He granted us dominion
O'er all the beauty He had made
We were worthy in His opinion.

We failed God right from the start,
We wanted our own way.
So the perfect Garden of Eden
Could no longer be our mainstay.

And, so it was, man was cast out
To live by the sweat of his brow;
Facing sickness, sorrow and even death,
Oftimes not knowing how.

God sent His Son to save us
From the sin that dwells within;
He empowers us to do His will,
To be ambassadors for Him.

He said, "Go into all the world,"
Take the gospel to every man;
Teach them Jesus loves them,
For each one He has a plan.

He directs us to Judea—
That's our own community;
Then out of town, to Samaria,
To uttermost parts, across the sea.

Feed the hungry, clothe the naked,
Welcome strangers in your midst;
Visit the ill and those imprisoned,
Turn your cheek, don't raise your fist!

Is God to Blame?   *(continued)*

He tells us that, inasmuch as
We serve the least of these,
We serve our blessed Savior,
Bringing to Him comfort and ease.

The church, too, is God's instrument
Gathering His people in one accord;
Sharing our joys and sorrows,
And doing the will of our Lord.

The Body of Christ together
Is capable of so much more;
Efforts of Christians united
Can reach from shore to shore.

Since we are only human
And can't see beyond today;
We question, doubt and travail
At whatever comes our way.

But is God to blame? No, we're to blame,
We are His hands, His feet;
We are His special instruments
And must His will complete.

Just an Earthen Vessel

Sometimes the day seems wasted
And rough and steep the road.
Sometimes I'm oh, so weary
And bent beneath the load.
Sometimes my vision's hazy
And my feet, they go astray.
Sometimes I do not listen
And cannot find my way.

Sometimes my hands so tremble,
My legs seem weak and frail.
Sometimes I can't get started
And know I'll surely fail.
Sometimes I have no feeling
Deep down within my heart.
Sometimes I fail to do God's will
And I fall down on my part.

I am just an earthen vessel
Formed from the clay and sod;
But, in this faulty vessel
Lives the Holy Son of God.
He paid the price at Calv'ry,
He rose to set me free;
And I can do anything
Through Christ who strengthens me.

Oh, marvelous, wonderful treasure
Deep down within my soul,
Reform my earthen vessel,
Renew and make me whole.
May others see Thy presence
As my vessel draws from Thee
Living water so refreshing,
Overflowing, rich, and free.

My Earthen Vessel

Sometimes my earthen vessel
It pains and aches me so.
Sometimes it slows and falters
And I just can't make it go.
Sometimes I want to do so much
And can't do anything.
Sometimes I have a song inside
But not the strength to sing.
My vessel may be tattered
And weathered by life's storm.
Its members may not function well,
It may have lost its normal form;
But, within my earthen vessel
Lives the precious Son of God—
A treasure incorruptible
With outreach deep and broad.
While my vessel's only temporal—
What you see must surely die,
My soul, which is eternal,
Will dwell with God on high.

My Savior Loves Me Still

On entering the sanctuary,
I sensed the presence of the Lord.
Holy, holy and perfect was He,
Seeking His children in one accord.

I felt so uncomfortable,
So imperfect my humanity.
My concentration was broken,
I was thinking only of me.

Like Isaiah on the death of Uziah,
My humanity came to light.
"Woe is me, I am undone,"
'Twas a dreadful, lonely plight.

His presence brought revelation
Of my failure to do His will.
And, 'though undeserving, made me aware,
My Savior loves me still.

Not to Reason Why

Gobbled one turkey to another
As he looked up to the sky,
"If I could only have my freedom,
With the eagles I would fly.
I'd really be somebody,
And you'd all give me the eye.

Then said his wiser brother
As he looked him in the eye,
"Now you'd look mighty awkward
Soaring in the sky so high;
And from exposure and exhaustion,
You would of a surety die.
Each to his own, my brother,"
He offered with a sigh,
As he strutted toward the farmer
Since his fulfillment now was nigh.

The moral of this story
Is not to reason why,
But to go about the job at hand
Since all must do _and_ die.
Elsewhere is mighty tempting,
Greener grass and bluer sky;
But nowhere is there freedom
From the sweet bye and bye.

Praise the Lord
(Lyrics and music written by the Lord and Mollie Pool
and dedicated to the memory of
Mrs. Helen Strahm on August 21, 1977.)

Peter stepped in faith upon the rugged sea,
Looking toward the Master, he walked so boldly;
But his eyes caught one big wave,
And he cried the Lord to save.
Jesus reached his hand and lifted him gently.
Praise the Lord! Praise the Lord!
Jesus reached his hand and lifted him gently.
Praise the Lord! Praise the Lord!
He is reaching down, my friend, for you and me.

Came a woman to draw water from the well,
Her heart so heavy, to her knees she fell.
Jesus told her all her sin,
Living water gave within;
And she ran to all her friends His praise to tell.
Praise the Lord! Praise the Lord!
And she ran to all her friends His praise to tell.
Praise the Lord! Praise the Lord!
Let us share the living water from His well.

Saul was after all the Christians in the land.
He had papers to arrest them in his hand;
But the Lord, He struck him down,
Took his sight and turned him 'round;
And Paul joined the mighty Christian army band.
Praise the Lord! Praise the Lord!
And Paul joined the mighty Christian army band.
Praise the Lord! Praise the Lord!
We are members of that Christian army band.

Praise the Lord (continued)

I had a friend who dearly loved the Lord.
'Though her body racked in pain, her praise outpoured.
Oh, she loved God's people so,
And her heart was so aglow.
Human shackles now are lifted, praise the Lord!
Praise the Lord! Praise the Lord!
Human shackles now are lifted, praise the Lord!
Praise the Lord! Praise the Lord!
All God's children will be lifted, praise the Lord!

One day we're going to meet them over there;
And, with Jesus face to face, we'll all share.
What a great day that will be
When the Savior we shall see;
And the family of God will all be there.
Praise the Lord! Praise the Lord!
And the family of God will all be there.
Praise the Lord! Praise the Lord!
What a great day that will be over there!

Submission

Lord Jesus, you know that I love You much
And I want to go Your way.
You know I opened the door of my heart
And asked You in to stay.

But, Lord, as I travel along the way,
Forked paths of life so confuse.
I stammer and stutter and stumble about
As to which path I should choose.

Then, proud of my own accomplishments,
Thinking I can choose for myself,
I follow what I label best
And put You up on the shelf.

And, of course, Lord, I'm so busy, You know,
There's not enough time in the day
To read the inspired Word of God
And to fall down before Thee to pray.

Also, Jesus, I'm one of those folks
Who doesn't give credit to Thee,
One who doesn't exert my faith
Or look beyond what I can see.

It's not that I don't believe, dear God;
I know You're such a power in me
That criticism could change to encouragement,
And from gossip you can set me free.

You can help erase disgust and complaint,
Jealousy, impatience and pride.
You can make me smile when I am hurt,
To forgive time and again when I'm tried.

Lord Jesus, take this life of mine
And mold it by Thy plan.
Lead me, guide me, help me,
As only through thee, "I can."

The Four "L's" of Discipleship

Listen to the voice of God;

Linger to know His will;

Love thy neighbor as thyself

Launch out His plan to fulfill.

The Good Shepherd

In the beginning, God made everything
Beautiful in its time;
Setting eternity in our hearts
As the steps of life we climb.

From the moment of our birth,
We struggle with the will of God.
Seeing other, more exciting things,
Opting wayward paths to trod.

This way, our thoughts tell us,
The sky is a deeper blue,
Flowers are so much brighter
And smell so much better, too.

Somehow, through the twists and turns,
We find ourselves lost on the road;
The burdens of life become heavy
With no help to carry our load.

Now the skies seem ever so gray,
The flowers pale and wan;
Our zest for life has diminished,
Our energy's nearly gone.

But God never, ever forsakes us;
He is just a prayer away.
So, when we reach up in faith,
There's forgiveness for every stray.

Jesus is the Good Shepherd!
Leaving the ninety and nine
He searches for the one lost sheep
And brings him back in time.

The Way of Love
Music

I came to Jesus, weary, sad, alone.
My heavy burden barred me from His throne.
I was His child, He saved me from my sin;
But I felt empty and unfulfilled within.

I lingered there to seek His perfect will.
Remembering well the cost on Calvary's hill.
I sought at length a special spiritual gift—
To preach or teach, so that others I might lift.

And then I heard His still small voice to say,
I will show you a still more excellent way:
This way is love, love always comes before.
The way of love will end your inner war—

Faith, hope and love—all gifts from God above—
  And the greatest one is God's great gift of love.

The "Who" You Are

Like the beautiful leaves of fall—
The creation of God's own hand—
Each a different shape and color
Beyond our ability to understand;

We, too, are all shapes and sizes,
Different colors and abilities, too.
Varied personalities and temperaments
Affect what we say and do.

God created the "who" you are,
With a purpose in His mind;
Your very nature yearns for Him
And for His will to find.

Whether your gift be large or small,
Up front or just in the pew,
Whether you reach a great big crowd,
Or just a chosen few,

Whether you plant a seed yourself,
Or fertilize and water the sod,
You're but a human instrument,
The increase is up to God.

So, in Christ, we who are many
Of one body become a part;
We discover just who we are
When we seek Him with all our heart.

There's a Great Day Coming
(John 3:16, Matthew 25-31-45)
Music

There's a great day coming
When the King shall claim His own;
And, with angels all about Him,
He shall reign upon His throne.

Before Him will be gathered
Every kindred, every land.
The sheep He'll gather to His right,
And the goats to His left hand.

The King shall say unto His sheep,
The faithful and the true,
"Inherit now the kingdom that
I have prepared for you.
For I was hungry and you gave Me food;
Thirsty and you gave Me drink:
I was a stranger, and you welcomed Me;
Naked and you clothed Me;
Sick and in prison and you came to Me."

"When," shall the righteous ask,
"Did we do these things for thee?"
"As you've done it for the least of these,'
You have done it unto Me."

The King shall say unto the goats,
The lukewarm and the cold.
"Depart from me, I know you not,
You're not one of My fold.
For I was hungry, you gave Me no food;
Thirsty, you gave Me no drink;
I was a stranger, without welcome;
Naked and you left Me cold;
Sick and in prison, you left Me alone."

When," shall the wicked ask,
"Did we fail to do for thee?"
"As you turned away the least of these,'
You have turned away from Me."

27

Unworthy

I lift my eyes unto the hills,
Before me lies what Thou hast made.
Fields now full await the harvest,
Bright leaves fall, then quickly fade.

Here am I, so unworthy,
Who am I that you care for me?
While I was yet a sinner,
You died on Calvary.
If I must wait 'til I am worthy,
I will surely die in sin—
Take me, dear Jesus,
And change my life within.

I lift my eyes unto the hills,
My help comes from trust in Thee.
Thy great love uplifts Thy children,
From chains of sin You set us free.

Thank you, God, for Your creation
Made to satisfy our needs;
But, most of all, my praise is lifted
For salvation by grace—not by deeds.

When God Speaks
Acts 23—28

Before the great Sanhedrin,
Thru Paul's God-inspired defense
Feting Pharisee against Sadducee,
He was rescued from a scene intense.

Through this perilous situation,
God stood near and spoke to His own,
"Take courage, as you've done in Jerusalem,
So you must testify in Rome."

Undoubtedly, these words of encouragement
Were Paul's dreams fulfilled;
But perhaps not just how he wanted,
Nor just the way he willed.

Trials and appeals finally led Paul
Toward Rome across the sea.
Violent storms rose about them,
And all men for their lives did plea.

God spoke to His faithful servant
Promising safety for all on board;
Paul must stand before Caesar . . .
Witness in Rome for the Lord.

Oft times when our God speaks
Words of direction to us,
We think we know all the answers,
Forging ahead with nary a fuss.

That's when we encounter problems—
Hurdles and unseen delays.
Suffering and hardship attack us,
We don't understand God's ways.

When God Speaks *(continued)*

Reviewing the history of Paul,
We note that he didn't look back.
His focus was on what was ahead,
Not footprints behind on the track.

Paul believed the promises of God
Regardless of the cost,
Counted suffering for the cause of Christ
As something gained, never lost.

As we sense the leading of our Lord,
We must know delays may occur;
Sufferings and hardships may befall us
E'er we reach our goal secure.

We'll arrive to where He's leading
In God's own special time;
Maybe not just what we dreamed.
Nevertheless, 'twill be sublime!

(Based on sermon by
Dr. LeBron Fairbanks, President
Mount Vernon Nazarene University—OH)

Depression

Are you feeling hopeless and worthless today,
Like life's not worth living for you?
Do you find it difficult to keep on keepin' on
The way you used to do?

Have your activities lost their flavor?
Are you weary most of the day?
Do you face insomnia throughout the night,
Want to sleep the daytime away?

Are you finding it difficult to concentrate?
Do former tasks cause you despair?
Do you avoid contact with friends or crowds?
Has a loss or trauma been too much to bear?

Answering "Yes" to the questions above
May mean you are suffering "depression";
There's lots of this "disease" goin' round,
It's not just a simple obsession!

If you seriously consider harm to yourself,
You may need the help of a physician,
Who may find your problem is physical,
And solve it with a helpful prescription.

If it's just "Charlie Brown Depression,"
There're eight ways to pick you up:
1. Find a true friend who will listen
      To what's filling your woeful cup.

2. Perform some exercises every day
      Keep that body a-movin' 'round!
3. Go outside, whether sunshine or rain,
      Enjoy earth's beauty, take in each sound.

Depression *(continued)*

4. *Pull up the blinds, open the doors,*
   Let all that sunlight be seen!
5. *Change your diet to healthy foods--*
   Less sugar, salt, alcohol and caffeine.

6. *Divert your attention from the negatives--*
   Do something you long to do;
7. *Avoid contact with negative people*
   Who're on a downhill rendezvous.

8. *And, last but certainly not the least,*
   Take time each day to pray;
   For God, who made you, loves you still
   And will guide you all the way!

(Based on sermon by Rev. Scott Farman,
 United Methodist Church Pastor—FL)

Holiday
Reflections

A Child Born for Us

For to each one of us
A child was born;
We celebrate His birth
This Christmas morn.

What think we of Christ
As we honor His birth?
What means He to us
Whom God sent to earth?

A "Wonderful Counselor,"
He's all powerful and wise;
The "Mighty God" created
The earth, seas and skies.

The "Everlasting Father,"
Is concerned with each care.
The "Prince of Peace,"
Quiets each fear and despair.

What think you of Christ
As you honor His birth?
What means He to you
Whom God sent to earth?

For to each one of us
Christ can be born,
If we accept His gift
On this Christmas morn.

A Room for the Savior

The Bible tells of an innkeeper
Untouched by human need.
"No room" for weary travelers—
Christ was born where the cattle feed.

2000 years later we're heard to say,
"How cold and cruel was he!
Surely he had some warm, soft spot
For this father- and mother-to-be."

I wonder, Lord, had I been there,
Would I have turned them away?
Yes, I know, that night is history now,
And I am living today.

Is that you, Lord, I hear knocking?
I'm behind in devotions, you say;
But I'm so busy with work and such,
"No room" to read scriptures and pray.

I know, you gave me some talents,
And I've failed to use them for Thee;
But others are so much better, Lord,
There's "no room" to use them, you see!

And, about the money for missions,
I refigured the budget this year,
You know I tithe and give what I can,
But there's "no room" in the budget, I fear.

Yes, Lord, it's been a long, long while
Since I called on the lonely and ill;
But my schedule is so full of things,
There's "no room" to do your will.

A Room for the Savior (continued)

The knocking's getting louder, Lord,
You've made me so clearly see—
The innkeeper's life is history now,
But I'm as cold and cruel as he.

Keep knocking, I am coming, Lord,
My life I'll set apart.
Come in, you'll find a warm, soft spot
Deep down within my heart.

I'll daily read your Word and pray,
I offer my talents to you.
I'll give whatever you may ask
And seek all your will to do.

I'll share your love with others,
I'll try to make them see—
Christmas is a day of celebration
For those who make room for Thee.

Alleluia, Christ is Born!
Music

Alleluia, Christ is born!
Come, worship Him this Christmas morn.
Alleluia, crown Him King!
Sing His praises, shout and sing.

Holy Child, God's only Son,
King of Kings, and Lord of Lords!
Alleluia, Christ is born!
Come, worship Him this Christmas morn.

All Hail, King Jesus

In the beginning God . . .
Always was and always will be!
Creator of everywhere and everything
Accessed in life by you and me.

He gave us Ten Commandments
Paving the way for a fulfilled life.
Loving Him and loving each other
Would save us much anguish and strife.

And, knowing our bent to sinning,
He sent Jesus, His only Son,
To be born of the virgin Mary,
That our hearts might to Him be won.

Angels proclaimed His arrival
To shepherds in the field;
High in the sky a brilliant star
Led kings to worship and yield.

Humbly He came, humbly He left
As he died for our guilt and sin;
Personal belief in Him as Savior
Brings much joy and peace within.

All we see, feel, smell and touch
In this universe God created
Speaks of His love for all mankind
And we're so glad that we're "related."

Alpha, Omega
Music

Alpha, Omega--the beginning and the end--
Jesus, Savior, Master and Friend.
Creator of everything on earth and heav'n above,
You left Your home in Glory all because of Your great love.

And here am I so unworthy. Who am I that You care for me?
While I was yet a sinner, You died on Calvary.
If I must wait 'til I am worthy, I will surely die in sin.
Take me, Jesus, and change my life within.

Awesome Manger Scene

How awesome that manger scene
In the City of Bethlehem—
Mary, Joseph and the Christ child,
God's creation all about them.

The multitude of angels declaring,
"All glory to God on high,"
To frightened shepherds in the field,
Who left their flocks to come nigh.

This heavenly gift, the Son of man,
Brought wise men from afar,
Who saw God's message in the sky,
And followed that wondrous star.

Accepting the gift of Jesus Christ
Brings new life to the heart of man—
God's love, joy, peace and hope
Are first fruits of His holy plan.

Strength He provides for each new day,
Helping us love one another.
Our gift to him is a broken heart
When we fail to honor our brother.

"God is love," His word describes,
He wants what's best for us all;
And our world will be a better place
When mankind responds to His call.

Behold the Lamb of God
Music

The angels sang, "Alleluia,
Let there be peace on earth."
Alleluia! Alleluia!
Behold the Lamb of God
Which taketh away the sins of the world!

The shepherds left their flocks by night
To find the newborn child.
Behold the Christ! Behold the Lord!
Behold the Lamb of God
Which taketh away the sins of the world.

Three wise men follow'd a bright new star
And brought gifts from the East.
Promise fulfilled! Messiah come!
Behold the Lamb of God
Which taketh away the sins of the world.

He saves from sin! He lives within!
Oh, praise the Son of God.
Alleluia! Alleluia!
Behold the Lamb of God
Which taketh away the sins of the world.

Chorus
Behold the Lamb! Behold the Lamb!
Behold the Lamb of God
Which taketh way the sins of the world.
Behold the Lamb! Behold the Lamb!
Behold the Lamb of God
Which taketh way the sins of the world.

41

Christmas Bells
Music

Christmas bells herald the birth of a child
In Bethlehem City, so meek and so mild.
The Calvary Road His footsteps would find,
'Twas born to bring new life to all of mankind.

What will you do with His gift so rare?
Can Jesus in your celebration share?
The Savior is tenderly giving His call;
He wants your heart, your life, your all.

Receive Christ's gift on His birthday this year.
He'll fill your life with peace, love and cheer.
He'll take away all your guilt and your shame,
For 'twas on the cross He bore all the blame.

Chorus
Christmas bells, Christmas bells herald His birth.
Jesus, the Savior, has come to earth.
Angels rejoice in God's Heaven above,
"Jesus, the Savior, the gift of God's love."

Christmas Cheer

Carols we're singing,
Church bells are ringing,
We've baking and shopping to do
To bring our friends Christmas cheer.

Young hearts are yearning,
As play parts they're learning,
And there's so much left to do
Before we begin a new year.

Emmanuel—God with Us

God's greatest gift to all mankind
Is called "Emmanuel,"
The "Savior," "Jesus Christ the Lord,"
And "Prince of Peace" as well.

God saw the need of man's lost soul
Caused by our bent to sin,
And gave His only begotten Son
To come and abide within.

"Emmanuel" means "God with us"—
In the heart and by the side
Of those who, by faith, accept Him
And invite him to reside.

His abiding presence enables us
To have a brighter smile;
To go about our daily tasks
More joyful all the while.

He helps us love the unlovely,
To show patience and to be kind;
And our love deepens for each other
As His love conquers our mind.

Commitment we find more binding,
Devotion, more sincere;
God pricks our hearts when others hurt
And spurs us to help calm their fear.

He gives strength to live every day,
Comfort for every sorrow;
And, when He sees the falling tear,
Gives hope for each tomorrow.

Oh, "Lord" and "Savior," "Prince of Peace,"
Our dear "Emmanuel,,"
We praise you for your gift of love
As we ring the Christmas bell.

Every Knee Shall Bow

God knew when He sent His beloved Son
By a miraculous, virgin birth,
Mankind needed a Savior,
Peace and good will on earth.

Forgiveness He gives to the sinful heart,
Eternal life to the human soul.
He comforts each pain and sorrow,
Through Him, we are well and whole.

Many scoff at the power of His presence,
Celebrate His birth, but not the King;
Lavish the earth and all that's in it,
Eat, drink, are merry, and sing.

But He's coming some day to claim His own.
One great Christmas that will be,
When all people are gathered together
And the Savior we all shall see.

God exalted Him to the highest place,
Named Him above every name;
That, at the name of Jesus,
All people will bow the same,

In heaven, on earth and under the earth,
We'll all be in one accord,
As every tongue confesses
That Jesus Christ is Lord!

(Paraphrased from Philippians 2:9-11)

For God So Loved that He Gave . . .

When we take time to consider
The heavens, the work of God's hands,
The sun, the moon and all the stars
Made for all people of all lands.

Who are we, that God cares for us,
Giving us His beloved Son;
And why did He give us dominion
O'er all creation when day was done?

How excellent is Thy name, O Lord,
Our Lord, in all the earth!
From glorious reign in heaven above
To a lowly, humble birth.

You walked on earth as we must walk,
Acquainted with sorrow and grief.
You knew both love and rejection,
Crucified with a robber and thief.

You gave Your life that we might live
An abundant life full and free.
You provided for us a master plan
To live together in harmony.

Such love is unimaginable,
Such trust we don't deserve;
We've turned away from the One to whom
We should bow down, worship and serve.

May we know You, O Lord, more clearly,
Love You more dearly, we pray;
And follow You more nearly, *
This joyous Christmas day!

*Taken from Richard of Chichester's Prayer – Poem based on Psalm 8

46

From the Manger . . .

He was born in a rough-sawn manger
In a stable, to the cattle's low;
No room for the birth of the Savior,
'Tho the Heavens were all aglow.

A host of angels appeared to shepherds;
In the fields, they heard them sing;
Magi followed a star from afar
Leading them to the newborn King.

. . . to the Cross

God gave us His only begotten Son
To walk upon this earth,
To live His life as we live it—
Our senses, hopes, feelings from birth.

For all people who believe on Him
Jesus carried the old rugged cross;
Bearing our guilt on Calvary,
He willingly suffered the loss.

From the manger to the cross,
Thirty-three years of toil and strife;
God sent His only begotten Son
That we might have eternal life!

47

Love * Peace * Joy

Good Tidings of Great Joy

It's Christmas, friend, but all around
The world is troubled so;
Wars and crime surround us,
And we've no place else to go.

Fear not! For behold we bring
Good tidings of great joy . . .
For all the peoples of the world
God sent His only boy.

Within our hearts He can be born,
Wherever we may be.
This Savior, who is Christ, the Lord,
From sin will set us free.

And this shall be a sign to you
That He died upon the tree;
Willingly He suffered there,
My friend, for you and me.

Rejoice! Rejoice! For Christ is born.
He fills our lives anew.
Gifts of love and peace and joy
Are ours the whole year through!

Great Is the Lord

Great is the Lord and greatly to be praised!
>Who left His Heavenly home to become a man on earth;
>Who, by the virgin Mary, experienced a humble birth.

Great is the Lord and greatly to be praised!
>Who grew in wisdom and stature in favor of God and man;
>In the home of Joseph and Mary, grew to know His Father's plan.

Great is the Lord and greatly to be praised!
>Baptized by John the Baptist, was acknowledged by His Father above,
>As His beloved Son, who was worthy of His pleasure and His love.

Great is the Lord and greatly to be praised!
>Who chose twelve disciples to teach His purpose and His will;
>Who became obedient e'en unto death His Father's plan to fulfill.

Great is the Lord and greatly to be praised!
>Who, 'though crucified, dead, and buried, rose triumphant o'er the
>grave;
>His mission thereby complete that we, His people, He might save.

Great is the Lord and greatly to be praised!
>Jesus is the honored Guest—the Holy One born this day!
>Let us praise His Name together;
>Let us bow before Him and pray.

Have You Been to Bethlehem?
(Music)

Have you been to Bethlehem
To see God's Holy Son?
Have you heard the angels singing,
"Alleluia, Christ is come"?

Christ came two thousand years ago
To a land that's far away.
He's coming soon in the future;
And He is come today.

He's the Alpha and Omega,
The beginning and the end.
He lives within the heart of man
And becomes his eternal friend.

Come, my friend, to Bethlehem
To see God's Holy Son.
Come hear the angels singing,
"Alleluia, Christ is come!"

His Name Is Jesus
Music

" . . . and thou shalt call his name Jesus:
for He shall save His people from their sins. Matthew 1:21

Who is this Christ child tossed to and fro,
Born in a stable to the cattle's low?
His name is Jesus, God's only child,
Asleep in a manger, so sweet and so mild.

Who is this young man both wise and true,
Foreknew His mission—God's will to do?
His name is Jesus—lost from the clan,
In His Father's temple to seek His plan.

Who is this prophet, healer of men,
This loving servant beyond our ken?
His name is Jesus, who in God's will,
Laid down His life, the law to fulfill.

Who is this Savior, the Son of God;
Defying death—the earth, the sod?
His name is Jesus, He rose above,
Eternal life is His gift of love.

Make Room for the Savior
Music

Joseph and Mary, so weary,
Knocked on the door of the inn—
"No room," said the saddened keeper,
"No room" for the Savior of men.

Shepherds, frightened by angels,
Quickly left their flocks by night,
To find the Babe of Bethlehem,
To worship the Son of Light.

Three wise men were enlightened
As they spotted a foretold star,
And followed to bring the King of Kings
Precious gifts from the East afar.

Chorus
Make room in your heart for the Savior.
Come, worship the Son of Light.
Bring gifts to the matchless King of Kings,
As we, one-in-the-Spirit, unite.

More than a Babe

More than a Babe in a lowly stable
Heralded by angels to shepherds in the field.
More than a tiny King proclaimed by the Star
To three wise men who brought gifts and kneeled.

ANNOUNCING!
The birthday of our best friend!
Born to die for you and me.
God's greatest gift to all mankind
Bringing salvation full and free.

ANNOUNCING!
The birthday of our dearest friend,
Who walks with us day by day.
Who shares our joys and sorrows,
Giving strength along life's way.

May we receive God's gift to us,
With humble prayer and adoration—
Come, let us worship and adore Him,
In our Christmas celebration.

No Room in the Inn

Mary and Joseph were weary
On the long road to Bethlehem;
And, arriving in that crowded city,
Found no room for them in the inn.

It was in a lowly stable
They found shelter for the night,
Where Mary birthed God's only Son
'Neath the heavenly star so bright.

The Holy Child, wrapped in rags,
Lay in a manger for a bed,
With no family or friends to greet Him,
Only strange shepherds by angels led.

'Twas a hard world into which Christ was born,
Where King Herod sought for His life.
He faced suffering and danger daily
In a world full of hatred and strife.

More modern today but not different,
Our world is still much the same;
But to take us out of this wicked world
Wasn't the purpose for which Jesus came.

He came to give abundant life—
That's a promise ever so true;
But it's what he does within our hearts
That affects all we say and do.

His presence teaches us to love,
Be joyful and at peace.
He gives us strength to endure all things,
Gentleness, goodness, faith that will not cease.

He helps us become meek at heart
And temperate in every way.
He promises eternal life to those
Who follow Him day by day.

Jesus prayed to the Heavenly Father
We should not from this world be removed,
But He should keep us from evil—
And, by His presence, our hearts be soothed.

Good tidings of great joy we bring—
"Whosoever" means for "everyone,"
God so loved this sinful world,
He gave His only Son.

The Body of Christ

We are the body of Christ,
We are becoming as just one—
One love, one goal, one mission,
To serve Jesus, God's only Son.

We are brothers and sisters in Jesus.
Joys and sorrows we all share.
Our body reaches to strangers,
Here, there and everywhere.

We're the shepherds who left their flocks,
Wise men who followed the star.
We're the everlasting Body of Christ,
God's family near and far.

The Christ of Christmas

Christmas is not just a memory
       Of a night many years ago,
When God's Son was born in a stable,
       And slept to the cattle's low.

Not just a memory of Shepherds
       Abiding in the field,
Who left their flocks in the dark of night
       As angels the Savior revealed.

Not just a memory of wise men
       Who followed Bethlehem's star,
Bringing expensive gifts to the King
       From lands in the East afar.

The manger no longer holds Him
       And the star no longer appears.
God's Son was born to save mankind
       Down through eternity's years.

Christmas exists in the hearts of men
       Who invite the Savior in;
And know His love, and the peace and joy
       Of redemption from their sin.

The Christ of Christmas gave His life,
       His love to all He imparts.
He's very real to us today
       For He lives within our hearts.

The Christmas Quiz

What is the answer to this Christmas quiz?
Who do men say that Jesus is?
A prophet? Elijah? Great teacher? A king?
Why celebrate, give gifts and sing?

Many the prophets, great teachers and kings
Adorned in robes, gold crowns and rings.
Earth's mortal treasures too soon pass us by,
So soon forgotten, 'neath gravestones they lie.

For Jesus, the calendar names a day;
For Jesus, the whole world pauses from play;
For Jesus, schools and businesses close;
For Jesus 'tis done; for what reason, who knows?

Jesus is Christ, the Son of God.
No tomb could hold Him in the sod.
He arose a victor from the grave,
And seeks the souls of men to save.

What is your answer to this Christmas Quiz?
Who do you say that Jesus is?
Why do you celebrate, give gifts and sing?
Is He your Savior, your Master, your King?

The Greatest Gift

Soon and very soon
We'll celebrate Jesus' birth.
Many, many years ago
God sent Him to the earth.

He came here just to love us,
To show us how to live—
To be kind to one another,
To be thankful, and to give.

Santa helps us celebrate,
He makes us happy, too;
But Jesus is the greatest gift
God gave for me and you.

The Meaning of Christmas

"Merry Christmas! Merry Christmas!"
Joyous greetings from family and friends.
"We wish you a Happy New Year,"
Say the greetings that everyone sends.

What does it mean? Do we really know?
Can you tell what they wish for you?
Is it for fine expensive gifts,
Merry parties, gaiety, and much ado?

Is it a Christmas tree with lots of lights?
The ground covered with pure white snow?
Is it chattering and laughter of busy people
As they scurry to and fro?

Is it children sitting on Santa's lap
Telling him all they desire?
Is it beautiful street decorations,
Or stockings hung by the fire?

Is it the lovely Christmas music
Played in every department store;
Sung in church and by carolers,
As they gather outside your door?

Are we observing the birthday of Christ
Or fulfilling our own selfishness?
Is Jesus our guest of honor,
Or is His presence meaningless?

The Christ Child's birth was Holy,
For He's God's only begotten Son;
Born to die the supreme sacrifice
To atone for the sins of everyone.

The Meaning of Christmas *(continued)*

Can we then honor such a One as He
With selfish passion, lust and sin?
Does He not simply want assured
Of our love and service again and again?

And, isn't this very much displayed
In our treatment of mankind?
Have we compassion upon poor and needy,
The sick, imprisoned and the blind?

What can I give Thee, Master?
What can I do for Thee?
He replies, "Having helped the least of these,
Ye have done it unto Me."

The Real Christ Child

No room in the inn for the Savior,
But heaven would be His home.
No soft bed was His, just a manger,
But He'd ascend to gain a throne.

Born to just common parents,
But God's only beloved Son.
Performed the work of a carpenter,
But was the Messiah—the Holy one.

Crucified in early manhood,
He victoriously 'rose from the grave!
He gave His own life willingly
So that you and I He might save.

The Reason for the Season

On the first day of Christmas,
Great rejoicing resounded on earth
As heavenly angels appeared on high
Proclaiming the Savior's birth.

'Though born in a lowly stable,
He was announced with a brilliant star;
Shepherds left flocks to find Him,
Kings came from the East afar.

Gifts they brought to the newborn child—
For His kingship, bright shiny gold;
For His priesthood, fragrant frankincense;
Expensive myrrh His death foretold.

'Though not the king they had perceived
To wield power o'er all the land,
The Son of God had come to earth
To save the son of man.

Why do we celebrate Christmas?
Where's the focus on how we live?
Is Jesus our Lord and our Savior?
To Him our first love do we give?

Evergreens exemplify life;
Bright lights the heavenly star;
Carols we sing to proclaim His birth
Here at home and to lands afar.

The custom of gift-giving
Has an underlying reason—
Magi brought Christ their best offerings,
Which is the reason for the season!

The Savior Knocks
Music

It was night, they were tired from their journey,
So they knocked on the door of the inn.
"There's no room," came his words so distressing,
As he closed the door from within.
'Twas in a lowly, open stable
Where Mary birthed God's only Son.
The host of angels sang "Alleluia,"
In praise to the Holy One.

And so He knocks, "My dear child, may I enter?
Accept now God's great gift of love.
I am come to bring you peace and good will
And life everlasting above."

Shepherds left flocks in the field to find Him
And bowed at His manger bed,
Three kings from the East so wisely
By Bethlehem's star were led.
Jesus grew in wisdom and stature
In favor of God and of man,
And fulfilling the law and the prophets,
Gave His life to complete God's plan.

The Savior knocks, "My dear child, may I enter?
I am Christ, the pure Lamb that was slain.
I have borne on the cross all the sin of the world,
For your guilt I have suffered the pain."

And still He knocks, "My dear child, may I enter?"
But mankind must open the door.
Accepting God's gift of His only Son
Is what Christmas is really for!

The Supreme Gift

"Merry Christmas!" The birthday of Christ,
Whom God sent to this earth.
Through a peasant girl and carpenter,
Miraculous was His birth!

His coming wasn't to give us a cause
To eat, drink and be merry;
To overspend and overdo
For every Tom, Dick and Harry!

God's supreme gift was the life of His Son,
Laid down freely for man,
To save us from our wicked ways,
This was God's great plan.

The first Christmas, Christ was born
In the City of Bethlehem;
On Easter, He who laid down His life,
Rose to New Life again.

And God, Who gave His only Son
Graciously provides all things—
By the precision of the universe,
Life's offerings to us He brings.

If God, then, be for us,
Who can destroy His love?
No trouble, hardship or persecution
Can sever the tie from above.

Through Him, we are more than conquerors,
We're His body in one accord;
And, nothing can sever the love of God,
Through Jesus Christ, our Lord.

Thou Art the Christ
Music

The Son of God was born in a manger bed.
The angels sang, kings by a star were led.
This is the Christ, the Son of the living God,
The perfect Lamb to shed God's love abroad.
Good tidings of great joy they bring,
For this is Christ, the Savior and the King!

Jesus, our Lord, once walked with sinful man.
He asked in love, "Who do you say I am?"
Thou art the Christ, the Son of the living God,
The perfect Lamb to shed God's love abroad.
Good tidings of great joy we bring,
He is our Christ, our Savior and our King!

Tidings of Great Joy

Safe in the arms of Jesus,
Whose love will never cease.
Wonderful, Counselor, Mighty God,
Everlasting Father, Prince of Peace.

His teachings are for our highest good,
For the good of our neighbors, too—
Love, joy, peace and faith;
To be gentle, kind and true.

With Him, our joys are more joyful,
Love for each other deeper still;
He comforts life's pains and sorrows,
Gives strength for each valley and hill.

The birth of the Child of Bethlehem
Brought wise men from afar,
Who recognized the sign of God
In that brightly shining star.

Yet, He was announced to lowly shepherds
Tending their flocks by night
By a host of holy angels
In the heavens so light and bright,

Their glad tidings were for all mankind—
Rich or poor, great or small.
Come, let us worship this Christmas Day
Jesus Christ, who loves one and all!

Walk in His Footsteps

We prayed, "God, this year's been hard—
The road's been rough, life's climb so steep,
Our feet are sore, our bodies tired;
God, we often find it hard to sleep."

"I gave you my best at Christmas,"
God said, "Emmanuel is His name.
Born to live within your hearts,
To guide you thru' life's terrain."

"Precious children, take the hand
Of my only beloved Son;
Walk in the footsteps of the Savior,
He's the answer, He's the One!"

Who Is Jesus?

My Jesus is
God's only Son;
His precious Lamb;
The blessed Holy One.

My Jesus is
Creator of all things;
Omnipotent in His power;
The Heavenly King of Kings.

My Jesus is
Omniscient in His span;
Omnipresent on this earth;
Emmanuel—God with man.

My Jesus is
God's perfect sacrifice;
Redeemer of mankind;
Giver of life's price.

My Jesus is
Savior of my sin;
Counselor of my soul;
Comforter within.

My Jesus is
Everything to me;
All I will ever need
Throughout eternity.

Why Did You Come, Lord Jesus?

I came because sin brought to this world
Tremendous pain and sorrow;
Mankind living by the sweat of the brow,
And much worry for the morrow.

I came because sin brought to this world
Lots of enmity and hate;
And that, my child, was not God's plan
When He set out to create.

I came to give you strength from above--
Longsuffering in temptation and trial;
To teach you how to be gentle and good,
To walk with a friend the next mile.

I came to give you a lasting faith
When you lack understanding and hope,
To be a source for comfort
When it's difficult with life to cope.

I came to give you meekness
A quality in this world quite rare;
That you might relate to your brother
With great comfort and with care.

I came to give you temperance
As you partake of things of this world;
That o'er your own self you're in control
Regardless what t'ward you is hurled.

I came just for you, my precious child,
To fill you with life anew.
To provide a new beginning,
That you might God's Way pursue.

I came that you might have abundant life,
And not wallow in the throes of sin!
That you might know the source of love,
And have joy and peace within.

The Story of Easter
(Based on synoptic gospels in the Bible)

Jesus sat down with His twelve disciples
When the early eve was come.
'Twas their last supper with the incarnate Lord,
But they did not perceive . . . but for one.

The Master knew His betrayer well
As Judas asked, "Master, is it I?"
A moment of sorrow overcame His being,
"Thou hast said," was the Lord's reply.

Then came Jesus with them
To the garden of Gethsemane.
"My soul is exceeding sorrowful," He said,
"Tarry ye here and watch with me."

A little further He fell down and prayed,
As He felt the weight of man's guilt.
"My Father," He prayed, "Take this cup from me."
"Nevertheless, not my will but as thou wilt."

In agony He prayed more earnestly,
His sweat like blood dropped to the ground;
The disciples slept on and a multitude came,
His time had come, and He made not a sound.

Judas came forth, "Hail Master!" he cried,
His kiss was a token to betray.
Enemies with swords and staves were upon Him,
And His disciples fled as they led Him away.

Peter, following the crowd afar off,
Found a spot from which he could view;
But, as Jesus foretold, he denied Him thrice,
And wept as the cock in the distance crew.

71

The Story of Easter (continued)

Jesus was mocked, smitten and spat upon
As He faced His enemies through the night.
At the break of day to the Council was led
Where accusations were made ere 'twas light.

To Pilate's judgment hall they took Him,
Shouting and tossing Him to and fro.
Said Pilate, "I find no cause of death in Him.
I'll chastise Him and let Him go."

But voices prevailed, "Crucify Him!
The release of Barabbas we choose."
So Pilate gave sentence as they required,
And titled the cross, "King of the Jews."

Jesus, bearing His cross went forth,
But its weight he could no longer pull;
And they found a man, Simon by name,
Who bore the cross to the place of a skull.

Crucified there with two common thieves;
On each side one, His cross centered the scene.
His garments the soldiers among them divided,
Except they cast lots for His robe without seam.

Saith He to His mother and beloved disciple,
"Behold thy son—thy mother!" relating the two;
And, looking upon his killers, he pled,
"Father, forgive them, they know not what they do."

"Lord, remember me in your kingdom,"
Jesus heard among one thief's sighs;
And this thief heard the Lord's reply,
"Today thou shalt be with me in Paradise."

Soon they heard Jesus whisper, "I thirst."
One lifted a sponge to relieve His agony;
The ninth hour came, and He cried aloud,
"My God, why hast Thou forsaken Me?"

The Story of Easter (continued)

Darkness came—"It is finished," He sighed,
"Father, into Thy hands I commend my Spirit."
The earth shook, and they saw what took place,
"This was the Son of God," they had to admit.

Then came to Pilate a courageous disciple,
For the body of Jesus he made his request;
And, wrapping Him well in a linen shroud,
Gave his own rock-hewn tomb for his Lord to rest.

A great heavy stone was rolled covering the door
Of the tomb wherein Jesus lay.
It was sealed by the guard of soldiers
Who watched lest they steal Him away.

'Twas toward dawn of the first day of the week,
Two Marys came with spices. And, Lo!
The earth shook, and an angel descended,
With appearance like lightning and raiment white as snow.

"Fear not ye, for I know ye seek Jesus
Who was crucified," they heard him say,
"He is not here: For He is risen as He said,
Come see the place where the Lord lay."

New Life in the Spring

How exciting to watch God's creation
Come to new life in the Spring;
To joyfully welcome migrating birds
And hear them happily sing!

To watch the tulips and lilies
Push through the stubborn sod;
To know, 'tho we planted bulbs,
Growth is in the hands of God.

Something inside our beings
Is renewed by the earth in bloom;
'Twas Easter when Jesus was crucified
And rose from an empty tomb.

God so loved each one of us
He gave His only Son;
And as we believe in Him,
Our new life has just begun.

God Reconciled us to Himself through Christ

"From now on, therefore, we regard no one from a human point of view; even though we once knew Christ from a human point of view, we know him no longer in that way. So, if anyone is in Christ, there is a new creation: everything old has passed away; see, everything has become new! All this is from <u>God, who reconciled us to himself through Christ</u>, and has given us the ministry of reconciliation; that is, in Christ God was reconciling the world to himself, not counting their trespasses against them, and entrusting the message of reconciliation to us. So we are ambassadors for Christ, since God is making his appeal through us; we entreat you on behalf of Christ, be reconciled to God. For our sake he made him to be sin who knew no sin, so that in him we might become the righteousness of God." 2 Corinthians 5:15-21

For God so loved the world,
He gave His only Son;
His perfect gift to reconcile
Humanity . . . lost and undone.

Because Christ came in human form
To live on this sinful earth,
Laid down His life and rose again,
We can be of eternal worth!

We can be His new creation,
Seeing as His eyes can see--
The good and not the bad in men,
Not what they are, but what they can be.

God's perspective becomes our perspective,
God's will becomes our own;
With Jesus as our Savior,
We are never, no never alone.

We serve as God's ambassadors
To reconcile others to Him,
Because He sent His Son, Jesus,
"To be sin who knew no sin."

Thanksgiving Prayer

T hank you, Lord, for our friends so true.

H ear our prayer and bless them anew.

A ssure them their kindness is received in love.

N urture our friendship with Your bond from above.

K indle the flame of our Christian concern;

S how us the Way, with each twist and turn.

G rant us a passion Your love to share.

I nstill in our minds Your thoughts through prayer.

V isit us daily in the lives of our neighbors;

I nvite our service to their needs in their labors.

N estle us close as we hear You say,

"*G* iving to the least of these, you gave to Me today."

A Time to Be Thankful

It's the month of November
And a cool Fall day.
A time to be thankful,
Joyous, happy and gay!

T H A N K S
'Tis so easy to spell.
Why is it so difficult
For us to show and tell?

THANKS, LORD! T H A N K S

T is for the **truth** of thy salvation;
H is for the **hope** we have in Thee;
A is for **abundant life** made ready;
N is for **new life** so full and free.
K is for the **key** that opens knowledge;
S is for your **suffering** just for me;

Put them all together, they spell **"thanks,"**
A word we seldom ever say to Thee.

Reflections on Family

MOTHER

M aternity   made you my Mother

O bservation   molded my will

T heology   kept me in tune with God

H armony   said, "Peace, be still

E dification   brought needed improvement

R ejoicing   helped each task to fulfill

Because you willingly gave your time,
Because you had so much to share,
I can live this precious life of mine
Rejoicing, "There's a song in the air!"

What are Mothers Made of?

What are Mothers made of?
What keeps them on the go?
With what has God blessed them?
Wouldn't you really like to know?

First, to handle His gift of a child,
God made Mothers tender, meek and mild.
To relieve those many heartaches and fears,
He gave them buckets full of tears.

To share their awesome load of cares,
God made strong knees for daily prayers;
And, to comfort hits from area thugs,
Warm, cuddly arms for tender hugs.

God made Mothers able to nurse
All those cuts, bruises and even worse.
At bedtime, each little gal and feller
Knows God made her best storyteller.

Besides the endowment of unlimited money,
He filled her with joy and let her be funny.
God gave her an "inside track" as a cook,
No time to refer to that dusty cookbook.

A child loses nothing that Mother can't find,
She has a sixth sense to read your mind;
And, when you observe her eye a-winkin'
You know she knows just what you're thinkin'!

God gave her a long, sensitive finger
To make a strong point . . . or get out the stinger.
To avoid whippin', He gave her that "look"
For what wrong you did or thing you took!

He gave her a wide, forgiving smile
To let you know she'd reconcile;
But, most of all, the Father above
Endowed each Mother with a heart full of love.

Motherhood

Motherhood is special,
Brings out our very best;
Puts all the skills God gave us
Through the very toughest test.

God bless your celebration
As you give yourself a break!
Prop up those feet, lay down your head,
Relax for goodness sake!

A Mother's Prayer

I want my children to know you, Lord;
Help me to show them Your love.
Grant me Your guidance and strength, dear God,
As I reach for Your power from above.

We can't hate our brothers, you've told us,
To hate is as bad as to kill;
And, when we think or feel wrong inside,
We're apart from Your plan and will.

You taught us to walk the Way of Love,
Not of selfish pride and sin.
You gave Yourself as the ransom
That we might have peace within.

Use me, dear Lord, their mother
To show them that You are the Way.
Make my life Your example
In our home life every day.

"And this here's my baby!"

"And this here's my baby!" she'd exclaim—how I wish I'd early known
The value of being the youngest child in a family the size of my own.
I observed a beautiful picture unfold as I watched those early years—
Her brush strokes were both smooth and rough and stained by many tears.

The central theme of her picture is the Almighty Son of God.
To Him, she all majesty ascribes—ruler of sea, and sky and sod.
The little church by the side of the road brightly colors the scene;
And Mom is such a scholar, so the school can be clearly seen.

The home is quite simplistic, and there's an old Ford parked on the road.
Nothing fancy or unusual there—happy children, a dog, cat or toad.
Instruments of music are everywhere, their tones resound in the air.
Her persistent insistence for practice was a quality quite rare.

Along the path I watched as she strew sweet petals as from a rose;
I heard her pray ere she moved away, "May these aromas to them You
    disclose."
Petals of peace, joy, understanding, and thanksgiving to God above;
Truth, longsuffering, kindness, faith, hope, and most of all love.

Through every trial and tribulation, tranquility and hope prevailed.
She painted a living canvass, forgiving whenever we failed.
I watched and, with my dear mother, shed a tear and lifted my prayer,
"Please God, don't let me hurt her, let my life say, 'I care.'"

Why is this Mom super to the "baby" of our clan?
'Cause she's a beautiful picture of God's redemptive plan.
And, when I get to heaven, she'll introduce an older lady
To the Savior of mankind like this: "And this here is my baby!"

My Mother

You are someone very special,
You're "My Mother," very dear.
You're God's treasured earthen vessel
Filled with love, peace, joy and cheer.

When'ere I think of Jesus,
I know you led the way,
Teaching me the straight and narrow,
How to worship and to pray.

"May your day be filled with gladness,
May you sense God's presence there,
May you know how much I love you,"
This is my earnest prayer.

Thank You, Mother

Thank you, dear Mother, for being Christ's child,
For displaying His Spirit so tender and mild.
Thanks for being both genuine and true,
Always so interested in everything we do.

Thanks for your diligent teaching of truth,
For discipline firm in the years of our youth.
Thanks for the tears sometimes shed in vain,
As you watch your dear children in anguish and pain.

Thanks for the time that you give us in prayer,
For the knowledge you love us, the knowledge you care.
Thanks for forgiveness each time that we fail,
For faith that we'll soon get back on the trail.

Thank you for living a life filled with love,
Strengthened and empowered by the Father above.
From you we have learned we should love one another,
For you are our very own, wonderful Mother.

Parents' Anniversary Celebration
65 Years

Sixty-five years is a very long time,
Yet it passed in the wink of an eye.
Many memories you've made as years passed by,
Some made you happy, some made you cry.

This love has been nurtured, not left to die,
So it glowed, as the years grew long.
At times, just knowing the other was there,
Made it light, when things had gone wrong.

It's easy to see the respect you share,
The proud walk and the tilt of the head,
The pride in each other always displayed,
It is shared without a word being said.

The trust you feel is shared by others;
There is peace in the face of all strife,
For you count on each other whatever may come,
As hand-in-hand, you travel through life.

For marriage, you see, is a blending of souls;
With God's blessing, it long will endure.
For, if there is caring, and sharing and trust,
Then love will make it secure.

May the years be happy, as longer they grow,
May good health and contentment you find.
An example you are to the rest of the world—
You're in love, you're two of a kind!

An Evening Prayer

Oh Lord, the day's been long, the burdens great
As I've walked life's path today.
My parents are old, in failing health,
And I hardly know how to pray.

Since the very day of my birth
They committed my life to you,
Trusting you for my future,
Your disciples strong and true.

From your Word they taught, "If I'd put You first,
All things would work for my good";
And, Lord, You know I've followed the Way
Doing the very best that I could.

They taught me to trust You with all my heart,
Leaning not on just what I know;
In all my ways to acknowledge You
So You can my pathways show.

They raised me well, and I love You so;
Your plan has worked for me.
You've blessed my life, made me whole,
And to heaven given me the key.

Help them now to trust Your Word
As they've done o'er these many years.
May they recall how, through every trial,
You've wiped away their tears.

May they see that, as followers of Jesus,
Our resources are beyond this land;
That we have a Great Physician,
And we're in the hollow of His hand.

An Evening Prayer *(continued)*

You've promised Your grace is sufficient;
In our weakness, You have perfect power;
And so I commit their care to You
In this most difficult hour.

May they know, dear Lord, that I love them,
May they feel how much I care;
Most of all, may they know Your comfort
And sense Your presence there.

My Sweet Daddy

'Though your house has lost some shingles,
Weathered in the storms of life,
And your windows are dim and foggy
From much strain, toil and strife,

You're still that jolly, sweet daddy
Who hugged me in a childish game.
As birthdays come and birthdays go,
You'll always be the same.

90 Years Old and Still Fiddlin'

"Happy Birthday, dearest Daddy,"
A phenomenal 90 years old!
Wed 67 years to Leota Marie,
Fathered seven babies to hold—
Ferne Annabelle, Ralph Frederick, and Waneta June,
Ned Anton, Martha Allene, and Naomi Faye,
And then at last, and truly the least,
Came along little Mollie Rae.

They have been years of joy and happiness
As together we played and sang,
We'd make up most any music group—
Sweet heavenly, or country twang;
But the most beautiful sounds to your children's ears
Have been those of the old violin,
Lovely tunes so expertly played
Witnessing to God's love within.

Music has been the theme of your life
As you've lived to the glory of God,
Instructing your children in His ways,
A living example not sparing the rod.
These many years have been good ones,
Tempered with sorrow now and then;
But, through it all, the tunes flow on.
Now your ninety, and still fiddlin'.

Cookie's Silent Violin

Many years he stroked the bow
O'er his treasured violin,
Sharing the love of Jesus—
Peace and joy he felt within.

Filling his home with music,
Playing in the symphony;
But, most often it was in God's house
Where he fiddled so masterfully.

O'er his vital, spansive lifetime,
As he sought the Master's will,
He taught many a lad and lassie
To play melodies with skill.

Precious moments turned into minutes . . .
Minutes to hours, and then a day;
Days soon added up to a month . . .
Then to years, passing quickly away.

Fiddlin' that once brought peace and joy,
Laughter, and sometimes tears,
Faded into the twilight
Of Cookie's later years.

With fingers no longer nimble,
Eyes unable to see,
Body worn and decrepit,
His violin lies silently.

Although his violin lies silent
And age has taken its toll,
I can still hear my Daddy playin'
A-way down deep in my soul.

Two Brothers

Two brothers walked together
Amid life's toil and strife.
One's body was sick unto death,
And one's was sick unto life.

Said one, "Dear Lord, I'm ready,
My life I've lived for Thee,
Even so, come quickly, Lord,
From life's bonds now set me free!"

Said the other, "I am unhappy, Lord,
I will seek the pleasures of sin.
Watch over my wife and family,
But let me a new life begin."

Two sisters walked together
Saddened and lonely inside.
One's spirit could for love rejoice,
One's spirit for loss of love cried.

"Oh, Lord," the family daily prays,
"Help fill every lonely hour;
And lead back our prodigal brother
If it's within Thy power."

A Daddy like unto the Heavenly Father

As we gazed upon your tiny form
On the day that you were born,
'Twas with a sense of bewilderment—
"Are we joyful . . . or forlorn?"

"Dear God, what have we done?
Where do we go from here?
Guide us o'er his future,
For we tread this path in fear!"

"Heavenly Father, make him a Daddy,
Filled with 'agape' love, like thee;
And use us as your instruments
To model lives from sin set free."

God was faithful to His promises,
He was with us all along.
Through trials and tribulations,
He kept us steady and strong.

We're thankful you're a Daddy
Who serves our precious Lord,
Who, with your beautiful family,
Live for Him in one accord.

God's Harvest—Our Family

Just pilgrims we are on a journey
Our lives in the hands of God,
Who has given us many a blessing
And much harvest from earth's sod.

Three beautiful children we begat,
Now with families of your own;
The branches of our family tree
Have certainly strengthened and grown.

Yes, the years are passing us by!
Yes, earning a living makes you strive!
Yes, you're raisin' the next generation;
Yes, you're keepin' your family alive!

'Tis easy to see others are aging,
'Tho, when you look in the mirror,
Seems you haven't wrinkled quite as much—
Those crows feet are subtle and mere!

No, time doesn't stop for anyone;
No, it keeps marchin' on so fast.
It's important we treasure each moment
Making investments in things that last!

Taking time to smell the roses . . .
Watching the beautiful sun rise and set . . .
Listening to the sound of God's creatures . . .
Taking an interest in those you've met.

Meeting the needs of your family . . .
Paying attention to what they say . . .
Sharing God's love and a warm hug and kiss
At the end of the long, hard day.

As we old pilgrims still on life's journey
Reminisce as to what matters most,
'Tis the harvest God brought into our lives—
Our dear children of whom we boast!

Greeting Card Verses

For many years I have written verses and hand-designed all of our greeting cards. It has been such fun, and the recipients seem to enjoy and appreciate the home-made touch! The availability of graphics on computers is wonderful and enables the creation of some very lovely, attractive cards.

For this reason, I offer the following verses to be adapted or changed as needed for those who enjoy that kind of creativity and would like to utilize these verses.

Armor of God

It's been (number) years since that day

You made your commitment of love;

Here's a great recipe for continuity

Straight from the Father above . . .

Clad yourselves with the armor of God

To withstand what lies ahead--

—Girding your loins about with truth,

—The helmet of salvation on your head.

—Put on the breastplate of righteousness,

—Shod your feet with the gospel of peace;

—Hold out proudly the shield of faith

—For protection that will never cease.

—Take with you the sword of the Spirit,

—Which is the Word of God;

—And pray, dear ones, without ceasing,

—As these years together you trod.

(Paraphrased from Ephesians 6:13-18)

It Takes Two to Tango

It takes two to tango,

It takes two to fight;

It takes two to cuddle

Through the long, dark night.

We are made for each other

To love and to share.

God implanted a longing

For one another to care.

On this anniversary,

May you sense from above

God's presence and guidance,

And growth of your love.

Many Years

Your (number) of years is a very long time,
Yet it passed in the wink of an eye.
Memories you've made as the years went by,
Some happy, but some made you cry.

Your love was nurtured, not left to die,
So it flowed as the years grew long.
At times just knowing the other was there
Kept you going when things went wrong.

'Twas easy to see the respect you share,
The proud walk and the tilt of the head,
The pride in each other always displayed
And shared without a word being said.

The trust you share can also be felt.
There is peace in the face of strife,
For you count on each other whatever may come,
As hand in hand you travel through life.

For marriage, you see, is a blending of souls.
With God's blessings, it long will endure,
For if there is caring, and sharing and trust,
Then love will make it secure.

May the years be happy as longer they grow,
May good health and contentment you find.
An example you are to the rest of the world,
You're in love, you're two of a kind.

One More Anniversary

One more anniversary,
One more busy day in your life
Filled with so very much to do,
With so much stress and strife.

Oft times you feel so overwhelmed,
When will it all let up?
Does God fully understand
How much is in your cup?

Take a moment to seriously consider
How you face each precious day—
A gift from your Heavenly Father
Who walks with you each step of the way.

Deeply breathe today's fresh air,
Take time to smell the flowers;
Look for purpose in all kinds of weather,
Be it warm sunshine or showers.

Search out some special purpose
In the time you spend each day;
Choose to share with one another
God's miraculous shining ray.

Part of the Way

(Number) years is but part of the way,
But your love, dear ones, is here to stay.
Traveling low roads, and high roads, too;
To one another you've always been true.

May you sense in the celebration of your love
The presence and guidance of God above,
Who sustains and keeps you day after day
Strengthening your love that is here to stay!

Those Were the Days

Those were the days . . . sweet rendezvous;
So in love, just the two of you!
You'd gaze at each other . . . out over the hill,
All was so perfect, so quiet, so still.

No "rose garden" promise could you share,
Only the promise to love and to care.
The picture's changed, not so tranquil, serene,
But you've the strength of God on which to lean.

His promises keep those who watch and pray,
And guide every step from day to day.
So, we pray as you celebrate this year,
You'll draw even closer, dearer, still dear!

Two Bugs in a Rug

Hope you're as happy
As two bugs in a rug,
A-dancin' and kissin',
With many-a hug.

Keep the romance hoppin',
Keep the spirit alive!
Keep pursuin' and 'courtin'—
For fresh, "young love" strive.

Be courteous and attentive,
Gentle, kind and true.
Appreciate each other
In all that you do.

God's Word defines
The attributes of love;
Then He promises His strength
And power from above.

May you sense His presence
In your lives every day;
And know He will guide you
Each step of the way.

Two Peas in a Pod

Together now (number) years
And still two peas in a pod;
Surviving life's entanglements—
Tares 'n weeds 'n goldenrod.
So much out there to distract you,
So much could tear you apart;
But you've followed the Master's leading
To carefully guard your heart!
May He bless you this anniversary
And keep you in His care;
May you know we love and support you
And for you say a daily prayer.

Two Shall Be One

Says Paul in the book of Ephesians,
"The two will become one flesh."
In loving our spouse, we love ourself,
Thereby making our lives enmesh.

Thus, we'll feed and care for each other
As Christ feeds and cares for His church;
Gladly sharing our "everything,"
'Tis a profound mystery of worth!

The truest romance is formed . . .

When Friendship and Romance Meet

(Number) years have come and gone
Since your special wedding day;
A commitment that's stood the test of time . . .
Tests, trials and come what may.

Walking life's path together,
You've found how to be complete;
For the truest love is formed
When friendship and romance meet.

Years Come and Gone

(Number) years have come and gone
Since that beautiful (month) day;
So quickly it was here and gone,
So, too ,was the fading bouquet.

But, oh the treasures you have shared
O'er these years so quickly past,
Building family, home and relationships
That forever and ever will last.

May God continually guide you
As together you follow His way;
And may you know we love you much
And daily for you pray.

First Birthday

Happy Birthday, sweet (name),
On this your very first year.
We hope your day is full of fun,
Love, joy, and lots of cheer.

You know not of life's burdens,
You're blessed with simple trust
In those who love and care for you,
Who'll pave your path, or bust.

Please know we love you dearly
And miss your warm, sweet smile.
Perhaps we'll hold you close again
In just a little while.

We pray as time is fleeting,
And, today, you're one year old,
That God, in His great mercy,
Will keep you safely in His fold.

Happy Birthday 2

Happy Birthday, (name),
On this birthday No. 2.
Hope that you have lots of fun
Cake, ice cream and candy, too!

Sorry we can't be with you,
But we're thinking of you here;
And sending hugs and kisses
To bring you joy and cheer.

Mom and dad'll take you shoppin'
For something special with this dough,
Since we're unaware of your needs
But surely they will know.

In this box, besides this card,
You'll find a thing or two
To let you know we love you much
And care 'bout all you do.

Above all, we pray that Jesus
Will keep you in His care,
Watching o'er each step you take,
Whilst we are here and you are there!

Happy Birthday 3

Happy Birthday, (name),
Now you are three!
So hope you are happy . . .
Happy as can be!

Eat lots of cake,
Ice cream and candy;
Play many a game
Have a day that's just dandy!

(Relationship: i.e. Grandma & Grandpa)
Wish you much joy
And pray God's blessing
On our special young boy!

X O X O X O X O X
X O X O X O X O X O X
X O X O X O X O X

Happy Birthday 4

This year you can raise
All four fingers high—
One, two, three, four—
Such a fine little guy!

You'll have four candles
On your birthday cake;
So be very sure
A deep breath to take.

Here are four blue balloons
To make you smile,
Perhaps keep you busy
For a little while.

The four kinds of candy
You must eat slow;
Chew the gum well,
And please "Don't swallow"!

Wish we were there
To party with you;
To see how you've grown
And what you can do.

This card is full of
Hugs and kisses too—
X O X O X O X O
Happy Birthday, we dearly love you!

Happy Birthday 4

Uno, dos, tres, quatro—
One, two, three four;
Four fingers old today,
Four candles are the score.

Oh my, how you've grown
O'er this past year;
And what you have learned
Brings us great cheer!

(Relationship)* pray
For your peace and joy;
And a happy day
For our birthday boy!

i.e. "Grams and Gramps"

Happy Birthday 5

Sakes alive . . . (NAME) is five!
However can that be?
You'll be startin' kindergarten,
Footloose and fancy free!

Your house will be so lonely
What will Mom do all day
While you're learnin' readin' and writin',
Drawin' pictures and goin' out to play?

We wish you a "Happy Birthday,"
And wish we could be there
To watch you blow those candles out
And the cake and ice cream share.

Happy Birthday 6

From distant planet Phloog,
Space alien Narq, the blaster;
At disintegrating birthdays
He's one heck-of-a master!

And, for your birthday, (name),
He disintegrated year number 5;
Blasting smoke signals up into the air,
Six years (name) has been alive!

And so, he brings you six balloons
To blow up and blast away.
May your birthday be very "spac-ial"
As you celebrate and play.

Happy Birthday 7

You're blowing out seven candles this year;
And seven wishes we make to bring you cheer.

1. *Celebration with family and friends;*
   Games and activities 'til the day ends.

2. *Delicious cake and ice cream, too;*
   Lots of candy the whole day through.

3. *Something special to make your day full,*
   Like racing a car or riding a bull.

4. *May you receive some gifts today;*
   Perhaps some money may come your way.

5. *Seeing today all that you possess,*
   May you sense much joy and happiness.

6. *(name), you are one blessed little boy*
   For whom we wish peace and joy;

7. *And, most of all, may you know love*
   Of family, friends and God above.

   Wish (relationship) could be there
   That we might in your birthday share.

The Age of Eight

Hey, Grandpa!
What did we do at the age of 8?
Run around in the field,
Swing long on the gate.

Pick flowers for Mom,
Chop wood for Dad—
Skip out on our chores,
Then feel really bad.

Play a little baseball,
Perhaps some football, too.
Tag and hide and seek,
Just kids through and through!

No computers, no cell phones,
No I-Pads with games;
With Monopoly and puzzles
We kept busy during rains.

Our world's ever-changing
With every new year;
And we pray this 8th birthday
Is filled with good cheer!

May your birthday be special,
May the sun shine your way;
May you know that we love you
And for you daily pray.

Nine Steps

9

8

7

6

5

4

3

2

1

(name), you're looking pretty good,
You're appearing mighty fine!
You've climbed yet another step—
One through eight, and now you're nine!

We see you're havin' lots of fun,
Swimmin', fishin', horseback ridin', too;
And headin' this Fall to 4th grade,
A busy year in store for you.

We hope your birthday is joyful,
With plenty of cake, and goodies, too!
And as you celebrate this ninth year,
Please know that we love you!

Happy Birthday 10

You've conquered life's initial hill
When your first ten years are o'er.
The terrain is somewhat different,
You don't get teddy bear cards anymore!

Thinking more of the "whys" and "wherefores,"
'Bout how God's creatures live and die;
Caring more 'bout how things are done,
And what really will satisfy.

As you roam about the great outdoors
And look to the skies above,
We pray you'll discover the Creator
And His wonderful, endless love.

When facing life's difficult choices,
Unsure which way to shove or push,
Remember that "A bird in the hand
Is worth two of them in the bush."

Life's Race

"Jesus increased in wisdom and stature,
And in favor with God and man." (Luke 2:52)
At twelve he was found in the temple
Researching His Father's great plan.

Age twelve is time for transition--
No longer a child of innocence;
You've grown in wisdom and stature
With choices of consequence.

God gives us a grand proposition
Should we run life's race with Him.
Making choices through His guidance
Fills life's cup up and over the brim.

God teaches us to rid ourselves
Of all that entangles and ties;
He tells us to run the race of life
In such a way as to win the prize.

Life really is like a game of sports,
Or any other competition;
Training, dedication, perseverance,
All required for our best position.

And the race, God says, is not always won
By the most swift and talented one;
For time and chance have a lot to do
With our lot when the day is done.

(See related scripture verses on next page.)

". . . let us throw off everything that hinders
and the sin that so easily entangles,
and let us run with perseverance
the race marked out for us.
Let us fix our eyes on Jesus,
the author and perfector of our faith . . ."
Hebrews 12:1-2

"Do you not know that in a race
all the runners run,
but only one gets the prize?
Run in such a way as to get the prize."
I Corinthians 9:24

"I have fought the good fight,
I have finished the race,
I have kept the faith.
Now there is in store for me
the crown of righteousness,
which the Lord, the righteous Judge,
will award to me on that day . . ."
II Timothy 4:7-8

"The race is not to the swift
or the battle to the strong,
nor does food come to the wise,
or wealth to the brilliant
or favor to the learned;
but time and chance
happen to them all."
Ecclesiastes 9:11

Finally Thirteen

So, you're finally thirteen years old,
A real teenager, true blue;
Now you think you know everything,
There's nothin' you cannot do!

In one moment you're feelin' happy,
The next you're feelin' sad;
This hour you're aimin' to please,
The next you're behavin' bad.

You're growin' by leaps and bounds
Those hands and feet so big!
There's never enough food around
You're eatin' like a ravenous pig.

So much happenin' all at once,
The body's ahead of the mind;
'Tis the time for diligent study
For God's will to seek and find.

Let not your heart be troubled,
We've all been down that road;
And know the Lord is able
To help carry your heavy load!

————————

And Jesus grew in wisdom and stature,
and in favor with God and men.
Luke 2:52

Do your best to present yourself to God
as one approved,
a workman who does not need to be ashamed
and who correctly handles the word of truth.
II Timothy 2:15

When We Were Fifteen

When we were fifteen . . .
Grandpa, do you remember when—
58 to 60 years ago—
What were we doing then?

Were we fixed up chic and trim?
Did we have a pleasing face?
Were our outfits absolutely in?
Was every hair in place?

Now, dear special grandchild,
You've reached that awesome age!
On your fantastic teen years,
You've turned another page.

Out there wooing all the gals (or guys),
Turning many an eye;
When sparks of love are flashing,
You're suddenly very shy.

No, (name), we haven't forgotten,
We were actually dating then;
Will this transpire in your young life—
Who knows where or when?

Where Has Our Little Boy Gone?

There's no doubt about it,
O'er these fifteen years, 'tis true,
You've accomplished growth in stature,
And we hope in wisdom, too!

Oh where, oh where has our little boy gone,
Or where, oh where can he be?
With his short, curly hair
*   and his shy little smile,*
Oh where, oh where can he be?

Oft times we just hope
That time will stand still
To enjoy precious moments,
To take in the thrill.

Just this moment we have to share,
And all too soon 'tis gone.
We must treasure every moment
As though it's our only one.

As now you see in the looking glass
The frame of a well-grown man,
May God grant you true wisdom,
And may you follow His plan.

Sweet Sixteen

"Sweet sixteen 'n never been kissed" (??)
In your teenage rendezvous.
'Tho many gals may be awed by you,
To your own self be true!

Just bet there's a car bearing your name
Out there in the great somewhere;
And, when you drive it, dear grandson,
We pray you'll take great care!

To a very special grandchild,
Talented in most every way,
We wish you God's richest blessings
And a fabulous 16th birthday!

Flower of the Month

Like the lovely (flower of the month),
You continue to blossom and grow,
Each year still more beautiful
The more you learn and know.

May God grant you continued wisdom
As you venture forth from home;
May you sense His presence by your side
Wherever you may roam.

(number) years—that's impossible!
Swiftly gone with a wink and a nod;
But you'll always be our "grand<u>child</u>,"
And a child in the eyes of God.

Twenty-One

Happy twenty-first birthday!
Such a perfect age to be . . .
Adulthood, in charge, responsible,
Footloose and fancy free!

Now you can do what you want,
But what you want has drastically changed.
You've grown in wisdom and stature,
Your desires have been rearranged.

You've been nurtured by Godly parents
In the paths of righteousness;
And, in the steps of your Lord and Savior,
You'll know joy and happiness.

When you were a child,
You spoke as a child,
Understood as a child,
Thought as a child;
But, now an adult,
You've put away childish things.

The very best advice we can give—
Walk in the steps of God above;
Continually absorb I Corinthians 13,
Paul's treatise on faith, hope and love.

Life's not always a "bed of roses,"
We're not always on "Easy Street";
But our caring and loving Shepherd
Compassionately hears each bleat.

"This is the day which the Lord hath made;
We will rejoice and be glad in it."—Psalm 118:24
Happy 21st Birthday, (name),
May your birthday be EXQUISITE!

Patriotic

Rockets ascend . . . fireworks pop!
"Ahs," "oohs" and "sakes alive!"
The crowd stands in amazement
(Name) is forty-five!

Friends and family stand in awe,
Oh my, how can this be?
Still, seemingly, young and beautiful,
"Share your secret," is our plea.

Walk with Christ one day at a time,
Make each opportunity last;
And, on this birthday, especially,
May your celebration be a blast!

Forty-Nine and Holding

Forty-nine and hangin' tight;
Don't wanna make next year's hop!
Headin' for fifty ain't so nifty,
'Cause it takes you over the top!!

So just continue hangin' tough
And enjoy the forties for now,
Forge ahead, keep up the pace,
Make neat, straight rows with your plow.

May you have a "Happy Birthday"
Filled with much joy and happiness;
And may your 49th year on earth
Be one of your very best!!

Toast to a "Fifties" Friend*
*To be given with bottle of prune juice

"Fifty is nifty," they say
And "Half a century's a blast!"
That's fun to say before you're there,
But now the die is cast.

Life seems to be all turned around,
As we ponder the passing years.
In fact, it's so depressing
You could shed some awesome tears.

Remember when you'd crave a steak
But no money could be found.
You have the money now, my friend,
But the teeth are not so sound.

Remember when you wished for time
For recreation and play.
The factor of time has made a trade,
Now a decrepit body's in the way.

Remember when you dreamed of affording
A night out on the town.
Now the easy chair, paper and TV
Are the best entertainment around.

(Man)
Remember being flustered
'Cause you lost your only comb.
Now you're flustered when you're almost out
Of polish for your dome.

Toast to a "Fifties" Friend (continued)

(Lady)
Remember that first gray hair
You could pluck out with a smile.
Now your pluckin' days are over
And you primp a shorter while.

Remember once your mind recalled
Many-a phone number, street and town.
Now you're lucky to recall your age
Unless it's written down.

Well, don't you fret, "fifties" friend,
No use to rant, rave and fuss.
Just lean back in your easy chair
And have a drink on us!

A Losing Battle

Another year has rolled around
In the busiest time of your life;
Darting here, there and everywhere,
Adds to your headaches and strife.

As the age-old adage goes,
Just take one day at a time.
Do what can be done today,
For some things, tomorrow is fine.

As those candles keep on mounting,
You actually see less dust;
Cleaning everything, every week
Is really not a must!

So, stop and smell the roses
For too soon they will be gone;
Whilst you're so busy with this and that
And runnin' hither and yon.

As you encounter another year,
Burn your candle at just one end—
Cool down . . . slow down . . . relax!
For others on you depend!

All American Boy

We've always wondered, could it really be true?
Does that long-ago rhyme ring true about you?
You with your guns and your fishing gear,
Enjoyin' God's critters with 'nary a fear.

Trapsin' the woods, wadin' the creeks,
Gettin' ever so dirty from toes to cheeks.
Wearin' old jeans and worn-out shoes,
These are some of the things you choose.

Seems like the writer of this poem was wise,
He could see Little (name) in his eyes—
The ever so true, all-American boy,
Who brings to us all such happiness and joy!

Jesus said,
"Follow me, and I will make you
fishers of men."
Matthew 4:19

Battle of the Bulge

(Date) just keeps comin' 'round
As the clock keeps tickin' away.
And your age is that part of existence
From your birth up to today.

So what if you've existed a long, long time
And developed a wrinkle or two!
So what if the battle of the bulge is on
And you can't do what you used to do!

Just tell yourself it's gettin' better,
And better and better each year.
Such thoughts defray the agony
So you can smile and not shed a tear.

The power of positive thinking's
The real answer to life's game.
So have a "Positively Happy Birthday"
Make love, joy and peace your aim!

Birthday (Close Friend)

(Number) years have come and gone
Since first you graced this earth.
Your presence has enriched our lives
Like a gem of untold worth.

Each day you've walked this path of life
Strewing sweet petals along the way—
Aromas of kindness and peace and joy
From a lovely and colorful bouquet.

Through the many years we've known you,
You've become like a (relationship) to me;
And, while the miles come between us,
The feeling's as warm as can be.

So, have an especially Happy Birthday,
And know that we love you much.
We're delighted for your friendship,
To see you and feel your warm touch.

Birthday Suit

Remember what it was like
When your birthday suit fit?
Your skin so soft and super smooth,
Your hair full and exquisite?

As birthdays come and birthdays go
In life's progressive game,
We experience gains and losses
And will never be the same!

E-I-E-I-OLD!

(name) had a birthday cake,
E - I - E - I - O!
And on that cake were
(number) candles,
E - I - E - I - O!

With a puff-puff here
And a puff-puff there.
Here a puff! There a puff!
Everywhere a puff-puff!
So what is (name) known as now?

E-I-E-I-OLD!

Fragrant Flower

You are a beautiful, fragrant flower,
Colorful blossom formed by God's hand.
Your presence brings joy and contentment,
Purpose for living in this great land.

You are here for a particular purpose,
For you, there is a plan—
To serve as God's special instrument,
Showing His love to every man.

As you celebrate your birthday—
Party, cake and much ado—
May you know how much God loves you,
And that we love you, too!

House You Live In

Birthdays come and birthdays go
More swiftly every year;
And if we think too much of time,
We smother all the cheer.

Your aging human body
With all its aches and pains
Is just the house you live in
Bound tight with earthly chains.

While outwardly we seem to lose
Our youthful looks and thrust,
Our spirit grows more beautiful
When it's in God we trust.

Friend, you have endeared yourself,
As you keep on day by day,
To many, many people
Who've met you on life's way.

Joys of Autumn

Oh the joys of autumn
As we trample through the leaves;
Enjoy the fall sights and sounds—
Squirrels scampering in the trees.

Life changes all about us,
Trees and grass now fading green.
God has used so many colors
Painting us this autumn scene.

And He made it even lovelier
Gracing His earth with you;
You have touched the lives of others
In the things you say and do!

The years have passed so quickly,
Each one quicker than the last;
You've jumped right into senior-hood.
It happened all so fast!

As you celebrate this birthday,
Keep in mind God has a plan,
He put you here for a purpose
And He is your greatest fan!

Joys of Spring (or Summer)

Oh the joys of springtime (or summertime)
As we watch the flowers grow,
Enjoy the singing of the birds
Mating and nesting to and fro.

New life is all about us,
Trees and grass a healthy green.
God has used so many colors
Painting us this springtime scene.

And He made it even better
Gracing His earth with you;
Calling you to be His servant,
Guiding and directing all you do.

The years have passed so quickly,
Each one quicker than the last;
You've jumped right into senior-hood.
It happened all so fast!

As you celebrate this birthday,
Keep in mind God still has a plan,
He put you here for a purpose
And He is your greatest fan!

Joys of Winter

Oh the joys of wintertime
As we watch the pure, white snow,
Observe God's critters here and there
Scampering to and fro.

Nature all about us
Seems in slumber for the while;
We, too, snuggle in our covers
Facing the cold with a smile.

After winter cometh sweet spring,
There's hope with each longer day.
Every cloud has a silver lining,
Warm sunshine is on the way.

And God made the winter brighter
When He graced His earth with you;
You have touched the lives of others
In the things you say and do.

The years have passed so quickly,
Each one quicker than the last;
You've jumped right into senior-hood,
It happened all so fast!

As you celebrate this birthday,
Keep in mind God has a plan;
He put you here for a purpose,
And He is your greatest fan!

Life's Quilt

Your quilt now has (number) patches,
Each one an integral part;
Stitching together (name)
In God's timing, by His chart.

His design for you is special,
'Tho His ways we don't understand;
Just place every patch of your life's quilt
In the hollow of His hand.

Middle-age

You've passed young adulthood,
Old age is yet down the road;
Thoughts have shifted from "potential"
To "limitations"—what a heavy load!

Middle-age implies "resignation,"
Facing personal crises and strife;
Fearing inadequacy and failure,
Responsibility pressures in your life.

Look at it another way—
Life's neither beginning nor ending for you.
"There" is no better than "here,"
To your own self be true.

Pick up that bat, try once more,
As you taught your child to do;
Failure's just a step toward success
And God will see you through.

The opportunities are endless,
Middle-age is just the "between";
Stop to smell the roses,
Take time to enjoy God's scene.

On Age You Can't Ration

As time has it now, under regulation,
Add one year today . . . on age you can't ration.

You can wink at the boss . . . he might even wink back,
But don't let that throw you off of the track.

You can buy stylish clothes, follow latest fads,
Try stripes up and down, various prints and plaids.

You can dye the gray hair, cover wrinkles with junk,
Daily diet and starve to get rid of the hunk.

The beauty shop helps, perfume smells real good,
The cover-up's striking; but don't look under the hood.

That's the way it is—it's a fact of life,
The story of aging, of conflict and strife.

Forget it today, join your celebration,
Don't pain from hunger or from dehydration.

Lap it up and gulp it down,
Wear a smile and not a frown.

Have a fantabulous birthday!

One of the Classics

Happy Birthday to one of the "Classics,"
Now just what does that mean?
Well, (name), it suggests
You've lived quite long on earth's scene!

"Classics" were built robust and strong
With great style through and through.
Still putzin' around here and there,
Capturing the eyes of me and you.

Built to last, they ate plenty of gas
And ran for many a mile;
To get one today takes lots of pay
But brings one a happy smile.

"Classic" also means "high quality or grade,"
Absolutely "excellent" and "first class";
So we're sure you don't mind the reference,
Unless, of course, you prefer "Old Jackass" . . .

. . . and the donkey was before the "Classics"!

Seasonal Changes

Seasonal changes all about us,
Colorful leaves fall from each tree;
Creation undergoes God's awesome touch—
A panorama of His artistry!

Mankind is granted a number of years,
Our aging process slow, but sure;
We, too, change color, texture and shape,
Touch-ups help, but there is no cure!

At the tender age of (age),
You're still on the hill's incline;
'Tho the path becomes rugged and steeper
The higher that you climb.

The moral of the story is . . .
Take time . . . smell the roses a bit!
"This is the day the Lord has made,
Rejoice and be glad in it!"

What are Big Boys Made of?

What are little boys made of?
What are little boys made of?
Of sticks and snails and puppy dog tails,
That's what little boys are made of!

What are big boys made of?
What are big boys made of?
Guns, bows, knives and stuff . . .
There's never, never enough!

Of rabbits, deer and fish,
Many-a favorite dish;
But, when push comes to shove,
Most of all made of love!

What's in a Name?

According to Merriam-Webster,
The rose is a "prickly shrub."
It has very showy flowers
And a scent no one can snub.

Humanity, too is similarly housed
In a form we don't select.
We can't add one cubit of height
Or increase our intellect.

But, like the aromatic rose,
True beauty comes from within,
Surfacing in aromas of peace and joy
And love petals most genuine.

And you, dear friend (name)
Have lived true to your family name,
Producing the most sweet aromas
As you've made love your aim.

What's the Big Dill?

So you're havin' another birthday,
So what's the big dill?
It's not how old you are,
You've conquered each new hill!

So you're movin' some slower,
Can't rise from your favorite chair;
Can't read the newspaper
Or match colors that you wear.

So you're messy at the table,
Now and then you have a spill;
Can't see the spots anymore,
So, what's the big dill?

148

Winter

The wind doth blow,
The snow doth fly,
Another winter's here,
Another birthday's nigh.

Count last year's blessings,
But forget every care.
Life has happiness to offer,
And burdens to bear.

Live a day at a time
With its blessings or strife.
Today's the first day
Of the rest of your life.

Women and Mirrors

At the very tender age of eight,
A young woman looks and sees
A princess, perhaps Cinderella,
With the prince down on his knees.

A teenage gal of fifteen years
Sees Cinderella, Sleeping Beauty, too;
And a cute, popular cheerleader
Who no one can outdo.

At twenty, she sees too fat/too thin,
Too short, perhaps too tall;
She sees too straight or too curly,
Makes up, then goes to the ball!

By thirty, she still sees too fat/too thin,
Too short, perhaps too tall;
Still sees too straight or too curly,
No time to fix, just heads for the ball

Ms. Forty still sees too fat/too thin,
Too short, perhaps too tall;
Still sees too straight or too curly,
Says, "I'm clean!" and is off for the ball.

At fifty, a woman looks long and hard,
Says, "What you see is what you get."
Then goes wherever she desires,
No worry o'er her silhouette.

Women and Mirrors (continued)

A woman at sixty is happy to see
Her image, wrinkles and all.
Thinking of friends who can't see themselves,
She goes out and has a ball.

> At 70, she sees wisdom and laughter,
> The lighter side of life;
> And finds herself more at ease
> Despite others' discomfort and strife.

An eighty year old woman's philosophy is
"Just don't bother to look!
Grab your coat, put on your red hat
And get there by hook or by crook."

Congratulations!

Congratulations, (name),
You make us all so proud!
Here, there and everywhere,
We proclaim your praises loud!

Though the road has not been easy—
It takes practice, practice to excel;
You've surfaced a triumphant victor
And now you're performing well.

May God bless your continued journey
As you perform along life's way;
And may you know His peace and love
As you serve Him day by day.

Nine Wishes for the Graduate *(from Galations 5:22)*

You may be a doctor of medicine,
Racer in an astounding car;
Perhaps a renowned TV chef
Or missionary in a land afar.

Opportunities are endless,
Your talents are broad;
But you'll need these nine wishes--
Fruits of the Spirit of God.

Most important is the wish for **(1) LOVE**--
The very nature of God above.

A wish for **(2) JOY**, *whether you're up or down,*
Winner or loser, poor or renown.

In every situation, a wish for **(3) PEACE**,
For satisfaction that will never cease.

The wish for **(4) PATIENCE** . . . *a wonderful trait*
To slow you down and help you to wait.

A wish for **(5) KINDNESS** *to all you know,*
Whether this be our friend or foe.

A wish for **(6) GOODNESS** *to those in need,*
To share God's love in word and deed.

A wish for **(7) FAITHFULNESS** *in all you plan,*
Whether it be for God or for man.

A wish for **(8) GENTLENESS** *so very fine*
Is a beautiful strand in God's design.

And last, but certainly not the least,
A wish for **(9) SELF CONTROL.**
God blends all these gifts together
To refine our human soul.

Applying these fruits of God's Spirit
Makes our lives miraculous;
For then we desire to treat others
As we want them to treat us.

Today's Student—Tomorrow's Graduate

Graduation marks a certain finality
As you wander through the halls.
From high school you've climbed another step,
From within those very walls.

You're today's student – tomorrow's graduate
Sent forth to make your fame.
Things'll be different when you return,
They will never be the same.

As they bid you a fond farewell,
They desire that you should know,
It's not always an easy thing
To have to let you go.

A school is not just a building
Filled with desks and boards and books.
It takes a lot of people,
All shapes and sizes and looks.

You become kind of a family,
Sharing talents and abilities.
They hope those who leave their number
Can face life's realities.

You've been encouraged to set some goals
To reach as the years come and go;
And they hope you've come to understand
You'll reap just what you sow.

Who Am I?

EIGHT WEEKS
I'm a tiny fetus,
A yet unborn human life;
The offspring of (Dad's name)
And (Mom's name), his lovely wife.

TWELVE WEEKS
I am a little body
With tiny fingers and toes,
A heart that beats incessantly,
And eyes, ears, mouth and nose.

SIXTEEN WEEKS
I weigh perhaps four ounces—
Your size shows some contrast.
I hope you feel me move around
As my skeleton develops so fast.

TWENTY WEEKS
My wee little bones are hardening,
And I can grasp with my tiny hand.
I now have hair and eyebrows,
And my heart sounds really grand.

TWENTY-FOUR WEEKS
I am a "miniature baby"
With quite red wrinkled skin.
I sleep and move this way and that
To find comfort from within.

TWENTY-EIGHT WEEKS
My breathing system's developed,
My central nervous system, too.
I open and close my eyelids,
Hoping soon that I'll see you.

THIRTY-TWO WEEKS
I'm putting on some serious weight
As you can readily tell;
I'm standing on my head in here
And soon plan to rebel.

THIRTY-SIX WEEKS
I am a full grown baby now,
My lungs need exercise.
Any day's OK with me,
But I'll make it a real surprise.

SURPRISE!
My birthday time has finally come,
Mom and Dad, I'm so relieved.
Thanks for giving me my life,
For allowing me to be conceived

Welcome New Baby to Family

Welcome, (name), to the clan,
Congratulations Mom and Dad!
We're glad to have you on our team,
Such a handsome-looking lad.

God has His mark upon your life,
You're prayed for every day—
For Him to watch each step you take
And guide you on life's way.

We know your parents love you,
And God loves you even more;
For you He has a special plan,
For you there's much in store.

And there's a host about you
Of loved ones who really care,
Who, through all your ups and downs,
Promise to always be there.

You're a treasured earthen vessel,
A gift from God above.
The "clan" will watch over you
And teach you of God's love.

May God provide the strength each day
For your Mama and Papa, too;
The patience, kindness and longsuffering,
As only God can do.

The "clan" heralds your arrival,
Thanking our precious Lord above,
For your arrival, (name),
A gift of God and His love.

Even in the Valley

As I walk this life with the Shepherd
To still waters and pastures green,
He lovingly restores my soul
Making righteousness my life's theme.

I rejoice with Him in the good times—
Life's happy moments we joyfully share;
But, even in the valley,
My Shepherd is always there.

The Shepherd lifts me to new heights,
Knows my name and hears each prayer;
And, even in the valley,
My Shepherd is always there.

Death's by divine appointment—
All new life must one day die.
To Christ's child, death's but a shadow—
Sleep, departure, rest, good-bye.

I'll depart this life with my Shepherd
To the home prepared for me;
Forever to rest in green pastures,
Pure of heart, from sin set free.

God Knows

God knows your heavy heartache,

He sees the falling tear.

He gave His Son, Christ Jesus,

To lift you from your fear.

Just put your trust in Jesus,

Go to Him in earnest prayer.

There's comfort for your sorrow

And healing for you there.

Please know our prayers support you

As you face each passing day;

And remember, behind every cloud

There comes a shining ray.

God's Blessed Peace

As we gaze upon the glassy sea,
God causes us to think of thee;
Of how He stills the storms of life,
Of His blessed peace in the midst of strife.

Hang in There

God senses our troubled feelings,
He can calm the slightest fear;
He cares when we are hurting,
He sees the falling tear.

God knows our every weakness,
He hears our earnest plea;
His strength is sufficient,
His love is abundant and free.

Each day I bow on my knees
    in prayer--
"Please God,
    help (name)
    hang in there!"

Someone Gives a Hoot about You

There's someone special in our midst
Who gives a hoot about you.
You're a product of His creation,
And He cares about all you do.

He arrays the lilies of the field,
And colors the grasses green.
He feeds the sparrows of the air
And paints earth's beauteous scene.

His Word says not to be anxious
Since He knows our every care,
And promises His strength sufficient
If we go to Him in prayer.

There's someone special in our midst
Who gives a hoot about you.
It's God, our Heavenly Father;
And please know that we care, too!

The Good Shepherd Knows

The picture of Jesus, the Good Shepherd, has guided you down through the years.
The warmth of His presence about you has softened your heartaches and tears.
Your life has changed,—much older now—more helpless and dependent,
   'tis true;
Dimmer eyes and hearing loss, painful arthritis has plagued you, too.

Life has proven most difficult with losses of those you love;
"Why, Lord, couldn't it have been me?" you pray to God above.
Your ability to serve has been altered; you're lonely, unable to drive.
You often have feelings of uselessness, looking for purpose to be alive.

Let me tell you, my dear loved one, such happens to you and me;
But our Jesus never changes—the Good Shepherd He'll ever be.
He's the Alpha and Omega—same yesterday, today and forever!
You're still cared for in His flock through calm or stormy weather.

He knows your every weakness, watches o'er you day by day;
And promises to walk beside you as you continue on your way.
We're called to encourage one another, strengthen each other in word and deed;
To be a unified body in spirit aware of our brother's need.

    God's grace we know is sufficient,
    And we know He's always there.
    Let us vow to support each other,
    In word and deed and prayer.

Reflections
on
Cloud of Witnesses

Cloud of Witnesses

"Therefore, since we have so great a cloud of witnesses surrounding us,
let us also lay aside every encumbrance,
and the sin which so easily entangles us,
and let us run with endurance the race that is set before us."
Hebrews 12:1

A stern primary school teacher,
Saw each child as God's precious jewel;
Ethel McCartney rode the church bus,
Gathering them in for Sunday School

Sweet, hunch-backed Clara Dixon
Lost her only son as a teen;
Her drunkard spouse was abusive,
Yet forever on the Lord she did lean.

Blind Gilbert Hood so faithful,
Huge Braille Bible book in hand,
Must've checked with Pastor weekly
To know which scripture was planned.

As a child I thought she was rigid
About Commandments and Golden Rule;
But Lovell Miller was right on track,
She was nobody's fool!

Funny man and lover of youth,
Shorty Whalen gave us his all,
Sharing his farm for hayrides,
And becoming the "Santa on call."

Clyde Pool taught teenagers well
And was loved by even the "thugs";
How I treasured him as father-in-law,
The squeeze of his hand and hugs.

Cloud of Witnesses (continued)

A second Dad and mentor,
I found in brother-in-law, Lowell.
Encourager of all my writings,
Pushing me to attain each goal.

While teaching Young Marrieds at Westgate,
Henry Ruegg endeared himself to us;
He had much wisdom and stature,
And o'er all made such a fuss.

The Von Ins, Roy and Dorothy—
Gave of themselves beyond belief,
That others might fulfill their dreams
And in life know some relief.

I can in no way cite them all—
The "Cloud of Witnesses" for me;
But I continually sense their support
To be the Christian God wants me to be!

One Last Goodbye
"Beyond the Sunset When Day Is Done"
By Mollie R. Pool (12/20/00)

Countenances fell as we entered his room,
Gazed upon his sullen face,
Listened to his labored breathing,
Knowing he had reached the end of life's race.

He acknowledged when I held his hand;
But, did he really know me now?
"I'm here, I love you, Daddy,"
Then I kissed his cold, still brow.

With no means of communication,
We did what he taught us best.
As Ralph played the beloved violin,
We anchored to the "Haven of Rest."

We played and sang his favorites
As we have done through many long years.
"God, let Daddy hear the music,
But not see our sorrowful tears."

I hugged my loving Mother,
Knowing she, too must be aware
This could be our last goodbye . . .
Our special "Sweet Hour of Prayer."

"Out of the Ivory Palaces,"
"Away in a Manger" so low,
One "Silent Night, Holy Night"
Jesus came to a world of woe.

One Last Goodbye *(continued)*

"O Come All Ye Faithful,"
"Hark the Herald Angels Sing."
Let us have "A Little Talk with Jesus,"
Glory to the newborn King.

"Joy to the World, the Lord is come,"
"Just as I Am without one plea";
"His Eye Is on the Sparrow
And I know He watches me."

"Amazing Grace, how sweet the sound
That saved a wretch like me.
I once was lost but now am found
Was blind but now I see."

Lifting praise to the Great Creator,
We sang "How Great Thou Art";
And "Nearer My God to Thee"
I felt deep down in my heart.

We've got a "Mansion over the Hilltop,"
No more chains of sorrow and sin.
A kiss goodbye, "God Be with You," sweet Daddy,
"Until We Meet Again."

Time had come to stop the music . . .
Time to leave Daddy in God's care;
He had granted our one last goodbye—
One last special "Sweet Hour of Prayer."

I Remember Mama
By Mollie R. Pool
In memory of Leota Marie Cook 6/8/04 – 7/16/03

I remember Mama . . .
> She governed an old fashioned home--
> Seven children under her command
> Dare not far from the homestead roam.
> Sometimes we looked like rag-muffins,
> Barefooted and dirty, 'twould seem;
> But skipping off to church or school
> We were well-dressed and sparkling clean!

I remember Mama . . .
> With her stripped stink-weed switch,
> Chasing we three young ones
> As we'd run, duck and ditch.
> She knew not how to be violent,
> Although we deserved it, I'm sure.
> She could just give us that look
> To obtain the necessary cure.

I remember Mama . . .
> Our haircuts done home style,
> Kinda like the mixing bowl type
> 'Twould last for a very long while.
> How she loved to dress us alike,
> Although the color might vary.
> That meant that the very youngest
> With that style became quite wary.

I remember Mama . . .
> In church, close by her side,
> Drawing simple little pictures
> To keep us occupied.
> How she loved the many precious hymns.
> 'Though she couldn't sing on key.
> In spite of our mimics and giggling,
> She was as happy as can be.

I remember Mama . . .
  The object lessons in Sunday School,
  Bible stories by flannelgraph,
  Exemplifying the Golden Rule.
  Her deep concern for missions,
  The boxes she packed and sent.
  On church and district assignments,
  The many long hours she spent.

I remember Mama . . . .
  The ultra-neatness queen--
  A place for everything . . .
    everything in its place
  Made an efficient family scene.
  She followed a plan of action,
  On each child a task was laid.
  No one escaped an assignment
  And no allowance was ever paid.

I remember Mama . . .
  An intelligent, scholarly one.
  Our English so quickly corrected,
  Our homework must be well done.
  Encouraging us to practice our lessons,
  To be involved in everything.
  Exemplifying true leadership skills,
  More fulfillment in life to bring.

I remember Mama . . .
  Speaker and orator, the best!
  Practicing aloud at her ironing board,
  Preparing for an upcoming test.
  Competing with the very young
  Through the W-C-T-U.
  Winning their highest honor
  Among the very few.

I Remember Mama (continued)

I remember Mama . . .
The many puzzles she would build,
The numerous contests she would enter.
To defeat she'd never yield.
Crosswords were a special delight,
Something to challenge the brain.
Bible study to dig for details
More depth of knowledge to gain.

I remember Mama . . .
Stretching the money so far.
'Though poor, we were well cared for,
And Daddy always had a good car.
She never worked outside the home,
But served as Daddy's right hand—
Making appointments and doing billings,
At piano action work she was grand.

I remember Mama . . .
Money was scarce 'twas true.
Daddy rarely had change for coffee,
So we kids shared a dime of two.
Christmas time was sparse but happy,
With always those calendars to send;
Socks, underclothes, a toy or two,
They just didn't have much to spend.

But what most I remember 'bout Mama
Was her "Priority Number One"—
That we might have a personal relationship
With Jesus, God's Precious Son.
She bequeathed to us a fulfilled life—
Strength and fortitude for each day,
The mindset to enjoy God's blessings
As we travel life's long pathway.

170

Ferne Annabelle Myers

In Memoriam
February 18, 1924 – September 18, 2012
By Mollie R. Pool

I remember my second Mama . . .
   Thirteen years my senior was she,
   Pointin' her finger, shakin' her fist,
   Second in command and authority!

I remember my second Mama . . .
   Always tickling those piano keys,
   When she wasn't helpin' in the kitchen
   Or scrubbin' the floor on her knees.

I remember my second Mama . . .
   All us kids in harmony,
   As she played those awesome chords
   And we shared as family.

I remember my second Mama . . .
   Married when just seventeen
   To my ideal husband, Lowell,
   My second Dad, too, was keen!

I remember my second Mama . . .
   Birthed Joyce when I was six—
   The younger sister I never had
   Added "joy" to my life's mix.

I remember my second Mama . . .
   Spent half my life at her place;
   From just being a playmate,
   To a babysittin', cleanin', and cookin' pace.

I remember my second Mama . . .
   Taught me how to be a wife;
   Many a chore I did a second time,
   She prepared me for adult life.

I Remember My Second Mama (continued)

I remember my second Mama . . .
  Family dinners in her home;
  Cooking was her next best talent,
  For food the kids didn't roam.

I remember my second Mama . . .
  Italian cooking her specialty;
  Lived with Italians during the War—
  My favorite was ravioli!

I remember my second Mama . . .
  I so coveted the talent she had;
  God had made her such a blessing
  As she accompanied dear Lowell and Dad..

I remember my second Mama . . .
  Many years on the platform her place;
  Filling the church with melodious music
  Peaceful expressions on many-a face.

I remember my second Mama . . .
  Said she always "played second fiddle,"
  She needed that extra pat on the back
  To boost her morale a little.

I remember my second Mama . . .
  How she grew closer to her Lord.
  As the years kept piling on,
  She was feeling in sweeter accord.

I remember my second Mama . . .
  Yearning for her Heavenly Home;
  No more loneliness, tears or suffering,
  No longer on this earth to roam.

You've Crossed the Great Divide

In Memory of Brother Ralph F. Cooke
February 22, 1925 – June 11, 2003

Cookie, you've crossed the great divide,
Your work on earth is done.
'Though we are in great sorrow,
Your victory o'er death is won.

God endowed you with great talent,
A master of the violin.
So happily you played and sang
Bringing joy to your friends and kin.

Oh, Cookie, you are terribly missed,
And, 'tho our tears overflow;
Precious memories and lingering music
Will serve to make our hearts glow.

The Little Sister I Never Had

Joyce's birth when I was six
Made a little girl's heart so glad;
And I treasured and enjoyed
The little sister I never had.

She brought new life to our family
In the throes of World War II;
While Daddy Lowell and Uncle Ralph
Served our country as men must do.

We kinda grew up together,
Never living very far apart;
Playing and sharing the stuff we had,
We became "sisters" at heart.

As a teen I began to babysit,
Spent much time within their home.
Where I was taught to cook and clean,
And earned some money of my own.

Such a talented "little sister,"
She inherited her family's genes;
And pursuing a career in music
Became a teacher of high school teens.

Many a musical did she direct,
Artistically and professionally done;
And many honors and accolades
For these performances she has won.

But more important than accolades
Were her kind acts and caring soul.
Looking to the needs of others,
"Loving servant" became her goal.

While Joyce's home-going at sixty,
Makes my heart so very sad;
I thank God for sharing His treasure
Of the little sister I never had

By Mollie R. Pool
In Memory of Joyce L. Froning
June 28, 2003

Eulogy to Step-Grandad, Artie

Our Father, who art in heaven,
Hallowed by thy name.
Thy kingdom come, thy will be done
On earth and in heaven the same.

Your blessings on earth are many,
More plentiful than a seashore of sand.
How great is thy name in all the earth,
Yet you walk with me hand in hand.

Thank you, dear Jesus, for Artie.
While no blood relation was he,
He's the only grandpa I ever knew,
And like a grandchild he treated me.

How I loved to sit down by his side,
Listen to the words he spoke.
How I treasured his sweet, farmerish smile
And the way he'd kid and joke.

Forgive me, Lord, but I'd try so hard
To make him love me best.
I'd work diligently to prove
That I was better than the rest.

I'd nestle up real close to him
And hope he'd hug me tight.
He wasn't much of the lovin' kind,
But a little squeeze was all right!

Thank you for the times, dear Lord,
When we were side by side,
Picking berries, or digging potatoes,
Or taking a tractor ride.

Eulogy to Step-Grandad, Artie (continued)

I came today not to grieve
The passing of Artie, oh Lord,
I came to praise you for a soul
Who deserves a rich reward.

Thank you for letting me know him
For earth's limited little while,
And for the knowledge I'll see him again
And recognize his gentle smile.

May we who love him so dearly, Lord,
Feel your comforting presence near;
And may we, like him, live a vibrant life,
Sharing happiness, joy and cheer.

Mom Pool

She looked after all her youngin'
Kept 'em fed, clothed and super clean;
And, if 'n they were to cross her,
She could be quite stern and mean.

Her priorities: God, home and family!
Her talent: one phenomenal cook—
Those cookies, cakes and candies
Family and friends couldn't overlook.

To us all she was extra special . . .
Classy lady and all that stuff.
We'll miss her 'til our dying days,
'Bout her we can't say enough.

Thank you for sharing our sorrow,
For saying that you care.
It helped to ease the pain within
Just knowing you were there!

Are All My Children In?
Dedicated to Kimberly, Don and Tom Martin
On the death of their Mother, Wanda F. Martin,
September 10, 1983

God said,
   "This is the day the Lord has made
   Let us rejoice and be glad."
   But her heart was very heavy,
   She was uncertain, confused and sad.

God said,
   "Trust in the Lord with all thine heart,
   Lean not to thine own understanding."
   But she held to life intensively
   As though something went wrong in the planning.

   She lingered and pondered these questions,
   "Are my chores on earth now done?
   Have I done the very best I could?
   Has my life's battle been won?"

God said,
   "You fought the good fight, you kept the faith,
   Your heart is pure within.
   Receive now the gift of eternal life,"
   She asked, "Are all my children in?"

God said,
   "I was hungry and you fed me,
   A stranger and you took me in,
   I was thirsty and you gave me drink."
   She asked, "Are all my children in?"

Are All My Children In? *(continued)*

God said,
    "I was naked and you clothed me,
    You came to the prison so dim,
    You visited me when I was sick,"
    She asked, "Are all my children in?"

God said,
    "Come, my child, inherit now
    The kingdom prepared for you.
    The seed you've sown must needs be fed
    By other servants strong and true."

    So she took up her cross and followed
    Through Heaven's gates with Him;
    But the question we ask as his servants is,
    "Are all her children in?"

Thank You God for Aunt Opal

Thank you, God, for Aunt Opal.
We will miss her so very much—
How she cared what happened in our lives,
How she always kept in touch.

Having no children of her own,
She opened her heart to us;
Commended us when we made her proud,
Making over us a welcome fuss.

We've chuckled o'er these many years
'Bout her sweet, eccentric ways—
Her many pictures, gifts and trinkets,
Caring mementos of bygone days.

Each of our homes show forth her life
On a counter, shelf or wall;
And somewhere we've each a box or drawer
Full of family heritage to recall.

How we'll miss the occasional phone call,
Just thinking how we're getting along,
Or prompting that someone dear is ill
Or something has gone wrong.

How we'll miss her nervous excitement
As life's experiences she would tell,
Making each of us laugh and wonder
How she'd remember the details so well.

Thank you, God, for Aunt Opal.
Thank you so much for her love.
Forgive us for times we failed her,
Grant us comfort and peace from above.

(January 26, 1987)

180

THE HOUSE THAT JACK BUILT
(Jack Gibbs, Principal—East High School, Columbus OH)

The "house that Jack built"
Is not made with brick or clay.
It's not just a slogan on a wall
To read as you pass that way.

His foundation rock is the Golden Rule,
With respect both for self and mankind.
His structure is formed with living proof
Of wounded lives he helped to bind.

He gave the thirsty water,
The hungry a bite to eat.
He visited the sick and imprisoned,
And washed many weary feet.

Opportunity for all was his motto—
Education the key to success.
He spent his life for others
That happiness they might possess.

The "house that Jack built"
Will weather every storm.
His treasure will neither rust nor decay,
Nor will it ever lose its form.

The "house that Jack built"
Has changed the lives of man.
He's run the race and passed the baton;
Now he's counting on us to win.

A Forever Friend—Dorothy Von Ins
February 17, 1993

Young and impressionable when we met,
Dorothy was "truth" and "beauty,"
Fully committed to family,
God, country, and human duty.

Her children's teachers at public school
She supported with all her might;
Whenever Mary and Jim were involved,
Dorothy was well in sight.

How well do we remember "Teen Trips"—
The many projects to earn our way . . .
The trip we made together . . .
These thoughts cast a shining ray.

She watched our kids so we could go
To the young married couples' retreat;
We weren't the only ones she helped
As she served God with heart, hands and feet.

We watched as continually she gave of herself
In response to the "knocks on her door."
A ride, a meal, some clothing, a drink—
She knew well who was her "neighbor."

Our prayer has been o'er the thirty some years
That Dorothy's been our friend,
"Thanks for an honest, true Christian, God,
One who has helped our lies to mend.

"We needed an instrument of Your love
To cross our rugged pathway,
As she walked with You, sweet petals fell
Showing she was with You each day.

182

A Forever Friend—Dorothy Von Ins (continued)

"Please, God, let Dorothy know we love her,
That we'll visit her very soon.
This old world is not our permanent home,
For us, too, you've built a room.

"And help us, God, to pick up the torch,
And be a 'Forever Friend'
To someone along our own pathway
Who needs a helping hand."

ODE TO A FOREVER FRIEND—R. LYLE NORRIS
February 18, 1925—July 19, 2005

'Twas such an unlikely friendship,
At least at first it seemed—
Liberal Democratic vs. conservative Republican—
How could these two ever be teamed?

It began with Oyster Creek bowling,
When team-mates we became.
We opposites were actually compatible
And played a darn good game!

There was an occasional uprising—
The chance meeting at the bank
And the episode at Mel's Diner
Gave our friendship a hardy yank!

There were topics that we avoided,
Neither side could ever be swayed;
Yet we attended church together
As to God, the Father, we prayed.

And o'er the years that followed,
The bond grew deeper still,
As woodworkers shared their talents
Learning from each other's skill.

Many a meal we ate together
Celebrating birthdays year after year,
Sharing Thanksgiving dinner,
Bringing each other joy and cheer.

What fun we had at card games!
Oh, how he liked to win.
We can faintly hear the little "ahem,"
Transmitting a hint from him.

We always had each other
Through joys and heartaches, too,
We trusted his love and care for us
As no other friend we knew.

None of us know the trouble he felt
That caused him so much pain;
But we recall the wonderful man
Who enriched our lives again and again

Only once or twice in a lifetime
Are we blessed with such a true friend;
And so our hearts are broken
As that life has come to an end.

Lyle lives on through his wood crafts
Used in our home each day
And in the many fond memories
Of things he would do and say.

'Though but a very few years
Our pathways in life did cross,
We who've traveled life's way together
Are grieved by this tragic loss.

Ode to Nancy Kisel

I first observed Miss Nancy
With balls in her eyes in the sun
At Oyster Creek's swimming pool
Where we gathered for sun and fun.

The Kisels lived just down the street,
And soon became best of friends—
Golfing, bowling, partying,
Eating and sharing latest trends.

'Twas a joy to meet Miss Nancy
For an early morning walk.
I found 'twas doubly difficult
To keep up her stride and talk.

Both of us golf beginners
Joined O. C.'s nine-hole league.
Ere crossing the pond on Hole No. 1,
We already felt fatigue.

I recall on one occasion
We both hit a clump of trees.
When we managed to hit them two more times,
We fell in laughter to our knees.

With John gone for "the great flood,"
Nancy radioed an "SOS."
Phil peddled through wheel-high water
Putting his Schwinn to the ultimate test.

We got hooked on Beanie Babies,
Searching here, there and everywhere,
Waiting in ridiculous lines . . .
Whoever had them, we went there.

Ode to Nancy Kisel *(continued)*

Oh, the wonderful meals together—
Birthdays and holidays we'd share.
Somehow Nancy thought I liked carrots
And served them each time we went there.

After dinner we'd clear the table
To play our favorite games,
With prizes for winners and losers,
Couldn't remember next time their names.

Nancy brought us peanut butter cookies,
And they were, oh, so good!
We thanked her for her generosity,
Asked for the recipe, if she could.

Time passed by, we asked again,
She came knocking at our door
With another gift of cookies
And Betty Crocker mix for some more.

As years passed, we grew much closer . . .
More like a sister, not just a friend;
And I'll treasure that closeness in my heart
Til my own life comes to an end.